TExES

English as a Second Language Supplemental (ESL)

Practice Questions

TExES Practice Tests & Exam Review for the Texas Examinations of Educator Standards

DEAR FUTURE EXAM SUCCESS STORY

First of all, **THANK YOU** for purchasing Mometrix study materials!

Second, congratulations! You are one of the few determined test-takers who are committed to doing whatever it takes to excel on your exam. **You have come to the right place.** We developed these practice tests with one goal in mind: to deliver you the best possible approximation of the questions you will see on test day.

Standardized testing is one of the biggest obstacles on your road to success, which only increases the importance of doing well in the high-pressure, high-stakes environment of test day. Your results on this test could have a significant impact on your future, and these practice tests will give you the repetitions you need to build your familiarity and confidence with the test content and format to help you achieve your full potential on test day.

Your success is our success

We would love to hear from you! If you would like to share the story of your exam success or if you have any questions or comments in regard to our products, please contact us at **800-673-8175** or **support@mometrix.com**.

Thanks again for your business and we wish you continued success!

Sincerely,
The Mometrix Test Preparation Team

TABLE OF CONTENTS

Practice Test #1

Language Concepts and Language Acquisition

1. A middle school English Language Development (ELD) teacher is teaching English learners Greek and Latin roots. What skill is this teacher developing?

a. Phonics
b. Syntax
c. Semantics
d. Morphemes

2. An elementary school English Language Development (ELD) teacher has several Spanish-speaking students in her class. She knows that Spanish and English share many cognates, but she is unsure of whether or not to explicitly teach them these words in case she confuses her students. What course of action should she take?

a. Teach Latin roots to support students' understanding of language instead of cognates.
b. Do not teach the cognates, because there are many false cognates that will confuse the students. Instead, the teacher should focus on loan words.
c. Explicitly introduce cognates in Spanish and English while also including activities to show false cognates.
d. Read aloud a Spanish and English version of a story, and have students deduce the meaning of similar words.

3. An eighth-grade English language arts teacher is developing her students' persuasive academic writing skills. Which task would be most effective in supporting English learners' language development in this area?

a. Comparing and contrasting the vocabulary used in several different types of essays, such as narrative, expository, and persuasive
b. Analyzing the purpose and structure of several persuasive essay examples provided by the teacher
c. Watching a video on academic writing for essays that describes sentence structure, organization, and language register
d. Discussing in small groups topics for essays and writing first drafts together

4. An intermediate-level English learner from Japan has difficulty with pronouncing words such as "this," "math," and "them." Which reason best explains why he has difficulties?

a. The Japanese language does not use phonemes with the /th/ sound.
b. He has a language learning disability that requires extra support as these are fairly common Tier 1 words.
c. New English learners have a silent period in which they do not produce any English words but are instead absorbing the language auditorily.
d. English learners from all backgrounds often have trouble with these words because they are abstract concepts.

5. An English teacher for early-intermediate-level English learners from a variety of backgrounds wants his students to understand the subject–predicate pattern and subject–verb agreement for sentences. Which activity best supports this goal?

a. Comparing and contrasting sentences in English and Spanish for the English learners who speak Spanish
b. Reading English passages aloud with students so they can infer the sentence pattern from the passages
c. Explicit teaching of subject–predicate syntax through pairing students who arrange index cards, each containing a word from a meaningful sentence
d. Developing worksheets to be filled out by students individually that require students to practice subject–verb agreement

6. Students in a second-grade beginning-level English Language Development (ELD) class are performing actions while the teacher gives oral commands that are being modeled by the teacher such as "stand" and "jump." This is known as what type of strategy?

a. Total physical response
b. Direct teaching and mastery learning
c. Common underlying proficiency
d. Call and response

7. A high school science teacher notices that her English learners use informal language such as "you know" and "gonna" in their writing. What area of language should she focus on to support her students in moving toward a formal register?

a. Pragmatic competence
b. Morphological competence
c. Phonological competence
d. Syntactic competence

8. A teacher presents a lesson in which students in her English Language Development (ELD) class have paired up to come up with rhyming words such as "car," "bar," and "far." She focuses on phonemes from the English language that may not be common in other languages such as the /schwa/, /th/, and /r/. Each pair is given a word that they must find rhymes for and present to the class. What domain of language is she developing in her students?

a. Phonology
b. Syntax
c. Phonetics
d. Morphology

9. An elementary school class includes several intermediate-level English learners. Which activity is likely to be MOST effective in promoting their English-language development by encouraging communicative competence?

a. Students complete grammar drills that help them understand nouns, verbs, and adjectives.
b. Group students to practice role-playing a scenario in which students ask and give advice about school.
c. Students are asked to do a formal presentation to the class on heroes or heroines in their lives.
d. Assign an essay in which students must describe and explain a weather pattern such as rain or snow.

Refer to the following for questions 10–11:

A middle school social studies teacher has several Spanish-speaking beginning- and advanced-level English learners in his class. He pairs each of the beginning-level students with an advanced-level student to allow them to use their primary language to understand an assignment on ancient Roman history. The assignment culminates with a presentation on a famous Roman figure. However, he is worried that some of the beginner-level English learners will be too anxious to present in front of the whole class.

10. What factor affecting language development is he considering while worried about the presentation?

a. Background knowledge
b. Affective filter
c. First-language proficiency
d. Family acculturation

11. The group pairing is most likely to achieve which outcome for English learners in his class?

a. It will decrease the self-esteem of the beginning-level English language learners because they are intimidated by the level of English proficiency of the other students.
b. It will increase the assimilation of the beginning-level English learners because they are exposed to more advanced-level English speakers.
c. It will expand learners' understanding of the content because students are able to move back and forth from their first and second languages.
d. It will decrease the motivation of students to learn English because they are able to speak in their primary language.

12. A fifth-grade social studies teacher notices that one of her beginning-advanced English learners is having trouble with a unit on the American Revolution. This student is unable to write on what she knows about George Washington. Which factor is the most likely to affect second-language development in this context?

a. Psychological factors such as low self-esteem around language competence
b. A lack of prior knowledge of American history
c. Cultural factors such as not showing off what one knows
d. An underlying learning disability in memory or cognition

13. A middle school science teacher has taught a lesson on the different planets. Which follow-up activity to the lesson would be the best activity to promote classroom discourse that improves English language development?

a. Using a worksheet matching activity in which students identify the different planets and their features
b. Asking questions to the class while calling on students to respond, following up with an evaluation of the answer given
c. Quizzing students on what they have retained from the lesson for the teacher to see what topics need to be retaught
d. Using instructional conversation in which the teacher acts as a facilitator to assist students' understanding of concepts

14. A fourth-grade English learner has developed his basic interpersonal communication skills (BICS) fairly quickly since coming to the United States a year ago; however, his teacher has noticed that his cognitive academic language proficiency (CALP) is still behind other native English-speaking students. What advice would you give his teacher regarding his language development?

a. His teacher should be alarmed because CALP develops much more quickly than BICS.
b. His teacher should not be alarmed because it often takes 7 to 10 years for CALP to develop.
c. His teacher should refer him to get testing for special education services because his CALP is so far behind.
d. His teacher should expect his CALP to develop fairly soon, as it takes only 2 to 3 years to develop.

15. A high school science teacher has a group of beginning-intermediate-level English learners in her class. She has students answer questions regarding the parts of a cell and share them with the class. Which is the best way of lowering students' affective filters in her class?

a. Collecting all written work and correcting every mistake that students make regarding grammar, spelling, and punctuation
b. Having students work together in small groups to share their answers
c. Calling students randomly to give answers so that she knows every student is engaged
d. Not choosing any of the English language learners to give answers so they don't have to speak in front of the class

16. Read the sentence, and answer the question that follows:

This morning, I <u>eat</u> eggs for breakfast.

Students in a beginning-level English Language Development (ELD) class frequently make mistakes in their writing similar to the one underlined here. What is the first step that the teacher should take in addressing this problem to help students?

a. Teach verb tenses.
b. Distinguish between prepositions and appositives.
c. Teach the use of phrasal verbs.
d. Teach subject and predicate order.

17. Which of the following is NOT considered a dialectal difference?

a. Hindi and Urdu
b. Beijing and Hong Kong Chinese
c. New York City and Los Angeles dialects
d. African American Vernacular English and Southern United States English

18. Which of the following describes how positive language transfer can be used in the classroom to support second-language learning?

a. Allowing group work to enhance communicative competence
b. Monitoring errors in vocabulary and grammar in writing
c. Using dual-language examples in the classroom to teach sentence structures
d. Teaching common prefixes and suffixes

19. A first-grade English Language Development (ELD) teacher focuses on teaching grammatical features of English in a specific order. For example, he first teaches the use of the "–ing" verb form such as "walking." He then teaches adding "–s" to the end of regular third-person verb forms such as "She writes." What theory does this exemplify?

a. Interaction hypothesis
b. Affective filter hypothesis
c. Pivot grammar
d. Natural order theory

20. For a classroom activity, students are asked to interview one another about their interests. The teacher provides students with a list of follow-up questions and coaches them on how to show they are listening by using eye contact and nodding.

In this scenario, which language feature is the teacher focused on?

a. Semantics
b. Syntax
c. Discourse
d. Morphology

ESL Instruction and Assessment

21. A fifth-grade English language arts (ELA) teacher is determining which activity to use to develop his students' independence during reading. Which activity best achieves this goal?

a. Directed reading activity in which the teacher establishes background knowledge and arranges for students to read silently
b. Directed reading–thinking activity in which students facilitate their understanding through predictions
c. Explicit teaching in which objectives are clearly communicated and concepts are directly taught
d. Listen–read–discuss in which a text is read aloud with demonstrations and presentations

22. A middle school English teacher is planning a lesson incorporating Specially Designed Academic Instruction in English (SDAIE) for a group of early-advanced English learners. Which of the following would be most appropriate and effective to use with students at this proficiency level to promote their English language development in reading?

a. Simplifying passages being used so that when students read, they are able to comprehend the text and answer questions
b. Choosing and displaying language development objectives for the reading lesson
c. Avoiding texts with figurative language and idioms to support student understanding
d. Giving students organizers with blanks to fill in as they read to help them understand the passage

23. A 10th-grade math teacher has an early-intermediate English language learner in her class. She administers a math assessment on a unit on triangles that is predominantly comprised of word problems. What kind of test accommodations should she offer the student to address his needs while still assessing his abilities?

a. Give the student an open book test, so he or she can look up formulas he or she doesn't know.
b. Allow the student to ask questions during the test.
c. Reduce the number of words in the word problems so that the student only does the calculation portions.
d. Offer the student extended time to complete the exam.

24. Which of the following is not a component of using Specially Designed Academic Instruction in English (SDAIE) to design a lesson for English learners?

a. Teacher attitude
b. Comprehensibility
c. Interaction
d. Structured English Immersion (SEI)

25. A sixth-grade science teacher is designing a lesson that clusters students into three groups based on their needs: an intensive group, a benchmark group, and a strategic group. She is teaching the three states of matter. Which is the MOST appropriate activity for the strategic group to complete?

a. Students write a detailed explanation of each of the three states of matter using their textbooks and additional texts that the teacher has selected.
b. Students collect different materials that show the three states of matter and organize data listing their characteristics using deduction.
c. Students discuss different states of matter in a class discussion after watching a quick video describing the three states of matter.
d. Students categorize different materials into the three states of matter in pairs using visuals and charts.

26. Which of the following is appropriate for teachers in giving instructional feedback to English language learners (ELLs)?

a. They should include positive feedback as well as corrective feedback.
b. They should confine feedback to correction to avoid confusing students.
c. They should use feedback vocabulary above their level to motivate students.
d. They should avoid relating feedback beyond specific subjects to ensure clarity.

27. A sixth-grade math teacher considers several tools and strategies to use with her beginner-level English learners that would support their vocabulary development in math. She is specifically teaching surface area. Which tool would best serve this purpose?

a. A calculator so that they will not have to worry about making calculation errors
b. Worksheets with surface area practice problems
c. A page with pictures of three-dimensional objects and key terms that relate to these objects
d. A chart of essential formulas that they can use during tests and homework

28. The Texas Essential Knowledge and Skills require which of these as part of a K-12 foundation curriculum?

a. Social studies
b. Career education
c. Physical education
d. Technology applications

29. An upper-elementary school teacher is developing objectives for her lesson on indigenous plants of California. Which of the following would be an appropriate learning strategy objective?

a. To write in compound sentences using *and, or, so, but, nor,* and *yet*
b. To identify the characteristics of a variety of indigenous California plants
c. To use a Venn diagram to compare and contrast two different plants
d. To observe and record how samples of plants from California differ from alien plants

30. According to the Texas English Language Proficiency Standards, ELL students must acquire English language proficiency in:

a. Academic English language
b. Social and academic English
c. Social English language only
d. Neither social nor academic

31. The English Language Proficiency Standards of the Texas Administrative Code requires school districts to identify ELL students' English-language proficiency levels in which domains?

a. Reading and writing
b. Listening and speaking
c. Listening, speaking, reading, and writing
d. Reading, writing, and speaking

32. A third-grade English Language Development (ELD) teacher notices that several of her beginning-level English learners have issues with different skills. Which of the following is a cause for possible special education referral and is NOT likely due to external factors?

a. A student from a country where schooling was irregular experiences difficulty completing assignments and sitting still in class.
b. A student who recently immigrated to the United States and was separated from her parents exhibits failure to complete work yet wants approval from the teacher.
c. A student from another country shows difficulty with sound–symbol relationships and has difficulty connecting the alphabetic letters to the phonetic sounds.
d. A student has difficulty with remembering information across subjects even in his home language.

33. Before the start of the school year, a seventh-grade math teacher plans out how much time she will spend on each unit during the school year. She considers the English Language Development (ELD) standards that will be covered along with each content standard. What is this approach known as?

a. Backwards lesson planning
b. Differentiating lessons
c. Curriculum mapping
d. Holistic assessments

34. A sixth-grade math teacher is looking to implement a form of daily formative assessment to see what his students are still unsure of to reteach or revisit concepts that are unclear for his students. Which activity best fits what he is looking for?

a. A comprehensive test that covers all of the concepts from the unit so he can go back to reteach the concepts that students missed
b. Exit slips at the end of class with statements such as "I am still unclear about..." to check in with students
c. Homework assignments with several levels of questions that he can quickly check at the beginning of class
d. A mini quiz at the beginning of each class to prompt students' knowledge of the previous lesson

35. An 11th-grade government teacher has several advanced-level English learners in his class. He assigned an essay that must be written and typed at home. To write the essay, students must choose and conduct research online for one of the three branches of government. What should he consider when assigning this paper to his English learners?

a. Finding appropriate supports such as summary frames for their writing
b. Remembering not to assume that all of his students have access to technology at home
c. Letting his English learners choose a different topic so that they can discuss their own culture and government
d. Allowing his English learners to work on the essay during class while the other students complete a different activity

36. What is the primary difference between proficiency assessments and achievement tests?

a. Proficiency assessments measure a student's global language abilities, whereas achievement tests assess what a student has learned.
b. Proficiency assessments are given throughout the unit, whereas achievement tests are given at the end of a unit.
c. Proficiency assessments measure a student's grade-level placement, whereas achievement tests are standardized tests administered by the state.
d. Proficiency assessments and achievement tests are synonyms and measure the same thing—student achievement.

37. A middle-school science teacher and ESL teacher collaboratively teach a science class, introducing a science topic to ELL students using a semantic map containing many words related to the topic. Then they assign the students to create their own semantic maps for another science topic of their choice from the curriculum. Which skill will this most develop for the students?

a. Being able to differentiate fact from opinion
b. Classification and organization of information
c. Evaluating the reliability of given information
d. Predicting the outcomes of a series of events

38. A middle school drama teacher notices that one of his English learners is shy and often has difficulty participating in class. What is an effective, student-directed Specifically Designed Academic Instruction in English (SDAIE) strategy the teacher can use after the student speaks her lines during class?

a. The teacher gives explicit feedback to the students in front of the class on pronunciation.
b. The teacher writes down strategies for making improvements.
c. The teacher coaches students on positive self-affirmations.
d. The teacher reminds students to take deep breaths and rehearse the lines.

Refer to the following for questions 39–40:

An advanced placement physics teacher has several advanced-level English learners in her class. She is required to use a textbook assigned by the district based on what has been formally adopted by their state department of education. She gives a variety of tests including those that are provided by the textbook publisher.

39. What is the main benefit of using this test type as opposed to other types of exams?

a. It allows students to demonstrate their knowledge through a variety of means including using several different pieces of work by the students.
b. It is easier to grade, and the teacher does not have to spend time writing another examination.
c. It allows for authentic assessment of knowledge because students will have a chance to incorporate their own opinions.
d. It aligns closely with the state standards and the content knowledge required for the advanced placement exam.

40. She can best address the English learners' needs relative to textbooks in content-area classes with which of the following?

a. Give ELL students textbooks issued for lower grade levels in the subject.
b. Give ELL students condensed or summarized booklets as substitutes for the textbook.
c. Give ELL students the same textbook and provide L1 translations of key terms as needed.
d. Give ELL students visual graphic organizers and manipulative objects instead of the textbook.

41. A second-grade teacher with several beginning-level English learners is teaching her students how to create simple graphs to show data. She has a variety of resources to use such as visuals, realia, and websites. Which factor is the LEAST important when considering which resources to use?

a. The source is interesting to students because it includes technology, which engages them.
b. The content is accurate and up to date, including factual data regarding the class.
c. The context is relevant to her students, such as including culturally appropriate toys, foods, or objects as examples.
d. The resources appeal to a variety of learning modalities such as visual and kinesthetic.

42. An eighth-grade English Language Development (ELD) teacher pairs students during discussions and has the partners use error correction when a word or phrase is pronounced incorrectly several times. Several students in the class are intermediate-level English learners. What is an important limitation of using this method on a regular basis with English learners?

a. Students may not make the same mistakes over and over again, so no errors will be corrected.
b. It can be detrimental to student relationships with the teacher.
c. Overemphasis on error correction can lead to lower self-esteem.
d. Intermediate-level English learners are not advanced enough to conduct error correction.

43. An elementary school music teacher is introducing a new topic on string instruments to her students. She includes instruments common to the United States, such as guitar and violin, but she has also decided to include the pipa, a stringed Chinese instrument, and the sitar from India. Some of her English learners are from these areas. Which of the following describes the MOST likely outcome of this practice?

a. Interacting with familiar objects promotes English learners' language development.
b. Learning about instruments from other cultures will promote language abilities.
c. Teaching about these instruments will delay English learners' vocabulary skills.
d. Including these instruments will delay assimilation into the US mainstream culture.

44. A seventh-grade science teacher with several beginning-level English learners in his class considers how he can modify his speech to best support his learners. Which is NOT an effective modification of his speech?

a. Repeating key words
b. Using the primary language for directions
c. Simplifying the syntax of a sentence
d. Increasing his talk time for explanations

45. A 10th-grade English language arts (ELA) teacher has several early-advanced English learners in his class. Before reading a passage during class, students are placed into pairs to look for difficult words. They are then asked to apply different strategies to understand their meaning by using primary language cognates and morphemes. What is the reasoning for this activity?

a. Vocabulary acquisition helps support language acquisition and comprehension.
b. Skimming helps students develop test-taking skills for standardized tests.
c. Practicing cognates helps students identify which cognates are false and which are not.
d. Expanding their understanding of complex and compound sentences enhances language acquisition.

46. A seventh-grade math teacher considers how to use scaffolding to support her students in learning how to create a graph using a table. What is the first step she should take in scaffolding?

a. The teacher completes the task with student input.
b. The teacher models how to complete the task to students.
c. Both the teacher and student share the task duties.
d. Students try to complete the task on their own without support.

47. A teacher is creating a rubric to assess students' presentations on explorers around the world. She has broken up the scoring into several categories related to both language objectives and the standards for social studies. Which category does NOT relate to language assessment?

a. Content
b. Organization
c. Delivery
d. Fluency

48. A kindergarten English Language Development (ELD) teacher conducts a listening comprehension activity with her beginning-level English learners. She has them listen to a short, simple recorded passage. Which activity best fits the level appropriate for beginning-level learners?

a. Choosing between two written options to a question answered in the recording
b. Writing a sentence answering questions
c. Selecting an answer with the aid of illustrations
d. Providing a multi-sentence summary of what was said

49. A second-grade teacher is planning a unit on money sense for her English learners. Which of the following best describes a Task-Based Language Teaching (TBLT) approach to promote her students' language development?

a. Students create a chart with the differences between dollars and cents to hang up in class.
b. Students set up shops to sell different creations and use language to buy each other's products.
c. Students bring in actual money from their home countries that they can share with the class.
d. Students complete word problems that will be similar to those used on standardized assessments.

50. The English Language Development (ELD) department has asked teachers to calibrate the curriculum using a lesson they have conducted this week with ELD standards. What does this entail?

a. Seeing if the lessons include any ELD standards
b. Developing new lessons that fortify what was taught in the lessons this week
c. Considering how Specially Designed Academic Instruction in English (SDAIE) strategies have been implemented in the lesson
d. Assessing if learning activities in the lesson are aligned with the ELD standards

51. A middle school English Language Development (ELD) teacher has invited parents and community members to speak about their careers and backgrounds. What is the primary purpose of using this Specially Designed Academic Instruction in English (SDAIE) strategy?

a. Giving students a chance to ask questions to adults about their career goals
b. Establishing connections between the school and students' homes to promote achievement
c. Supporting language acquisition through listening to many different people speak English
d. Fulfilling the expectations around cultural diversity in the curriculum

52. In a written response, describe three ways to integrate and assess English language development (ELD) standards into subject-area instruction across the curriculum. Explain how each method would promote English language learner (ELL) students' development of both literacy in English and academic content knowledge.

53. Name three federal laws or Supreme Court decisions that affected English language learner (ELL) educational programs, and explain the impact of each upon such programs. Identify what each law or ruling requires educational agencies to do when implementing programs for ELL students.

54. Among the following scaffolding strategies to support student text interaction, which one is used only after reading?

a. Role, audience, format, topic (RAFT)
b. Question–answer relationships (QAR)
c. The questions-only strategy for reading
d. The reader's–writer's notebook strategy

55. When planning Specially Designed Academic Instruction in English (SDAIE) for middle-school English language learner (ELL) students with intermediate-level English language proficiency (ELP), which teacher approach is most applicable?

a. Integrating language objectives for content-specific structures and vocabulary in every algebra lesson
b. Giving ELLs more access to algebra lessons through skills and concepts at lower developmental levels
c. Putting off lessons involving more advanced algebra concepts until ELLs reach advanced receptive ELP
d. Planning lessons with minimal linguistic use, as math subjects rely less on language than others

56. Which of the following classroom techniques is MOST related to stimulating conversation?

a. Arranging the physical classroom space so students can see, hear, and reach each other
b. Using and displaying maps, artifacts, prints, puzzles, and similar content-related objects
c. Displaying and using various printed materials in English and students' native languages
d. Using all of these classroom techniques, as they are equally related to stimulating conversation

Foundations of ESL Education, Cultural Awareness, and Family and Community Involvement

57. Which of the following is an appropriate intercultural communication strategy?

a. Using Americanized names to make newcomers feel welcome
b. Using generalizations about cultural groups to know individuals
c. Finding out which terms cultural groups accept and using them
d. Maintaining the usual interpersonal space to show it is normal

58. A seventh-grade science teacher places diverse learners into groups that require cooperative lab work. She also praises times that students are able to work together despite their differences or when their differences bring multiple perspectives. What phenomenon is she seeking to reduce?

a. Social distance
b. Cultural relativism
c. Acculturation
d. Multicultural perspectives

59. An elementary school is preparing for parent–teacher conferences. Which of the following is NOT necessarily a consideration that the school and teachers should make with families of English learners?

a. Having appropriate interpretation services available
b. Being flexible for meeting times because some families work
c. Considering alternatives to in-person conferences
d. Providing refreshments for parents, so they feel welcome

60. As of 2023, from which country does the second-largest population of immigrants in the United States come?

a. China
b. The Philippines
c. India
d. Mexico

61. A seventh-grade social studies teacher is aware of his cultural context and understands how he was raised affects his perspectives. He understands the values of different cultures but does not necessarily agree with all of them. What is this known as?

a. Ethnocentrism
b. Ethical relativism
c. Cultural pluralism
d. Cultural relativism

62. To foster good teacher–student relationships between the teacher and all students, which action should a teacher avoid?

a. Convey equality and commitment toward all students.
b. Change the level of physical contact based on the student's cultural norms.
c. Allow students to discuss their feelings and personal lives.
d. Communicate acceptance toward all students.

63. A 12th-grade math teacher has a new English learner in her class. Ever since he arrived, she noticed that he tends to take longer than other students on activities and does not always adhere to the bell schedule. She thinks this is due to different cultural values around time. What is a modification she can provide for the student?

a. Change his schedule, so he has flexible classes.
b. Talk to the principal about this issue, so they can come up with a solution.
c. Allow for flexible timing of activities within her class period.
d. Pair the student with another student who can help speed up the work.

64. An elementary school puts on a cultural day in which students share their food, folklore, traditional attire, and games. Which of the following levels of multicultural education would this be considered?

a. Inclusive
b. Additive
c. Transformed
d. Exclusive

65. A teacher arranges students to work together into diverse cooperative learning groups. What is the likely impact of this action?

a. Students will have more conflicts because they may come from competitive cultures.
b. Students will develop semantic skills.
c. It fosters a culturally inclusive classroom.
d. It creates in- versus out-group dynamics that will divide the class.

66. Fahd is a 10th-grade student who shows signs of biculturalism. Which of the following would accurately describe how he behaves?

a. Fahd understands both Arabic and English but prefers to speak in Arabic in most cases.
b. Fahd feels ashamed of his home culture and only wants to speak English.
c. Fahd rejects American values and has strong ties to his home country and family.
d. Fahd easily switches back between English and Arabic depending on the situation.

67. A ninth-grade English teacher notices that one of her intermediate-level English learners tends to ramble in his written work. Before she writes down feedback regarding being concise and clear in his summaries, what should she keep in mind?

a. Because he is at the intermediate level, she shouldn't correct him so much.
b. His culture may use more storytelling in their discourse, which is reflected in his writing.
c. She should encourage his writing because at least he is trying hard.
d. She needs to try to give him feedback early on so that he is able to gain the skills he needs as soon as possible.

68. What is an important consideration when selecting diverse literature?

a. Is the author well-known to the students?
b. Does the book present stereotypical depictions of diverse characters?
c. Does the book include several different languages for students to read in?
d. Is the author still alive today and available for a talk at the school?

69. A second-grade English learner comes from a low socioeconomic background with parents who have not completed a middle school education. Her teacher notices that her parents are not involved in her schooling despite the class expectations that parents check over homework and read with the student. Which of the following explains why the parents do not get involved?

a. The family experiences cultural deprivation due to poverty.
b. The family is not interested in education.
c. The family holds different values on family involvement in education.
d. The family is uneducated, so they cannot read.

70. A sixth-grade math teacher notices that one of her advanced-level English learners from China is not excelling in her class. She is worried that this student may have a learning disability. Which of the following offers the best alternative perspective to this explanation?

a. The teacher has subscribed to the model minority myth.
b. The student is experiencing culture shock.
c. The teacher has not adequately explained the assignments.
d. The student has a language barrier that interferes with her learning abilities.

71. Race tensions at a middle school have risen due to an increase of Latino immigrants in the area. What is the best way to resolve conflicts and support cultural understanding?

a. Dividing up classes so each has a representative number of diverse students
b. Adding a mediation and conflict resolution elective course in the school
c. Increasing the disciplinary measures for racial intolerance at the school
d. Bringing in police surveillance to check for weapons

72. Which of the following best helps validate students' cultural identities?

a. Conducting naming interviews in which students learn about the origin of their classmates' names
b. Having a show-and-tell day in which students bring something that they are interested in to class
c. Focusing on author studies and the background of authors that students have read
d. Hosting a school field trip to a local museum with information on indigenous tribes from the area

73. A teacher is aware that several students in his class come from a culture in which girls are not pushed to excel in education. These girls in the class tend to be more passive. The teacher wants to encourage gender equity. Which approach is a culturally sensitive way to support the girls' education?

a. Speak with parents about how they are wrong in discouraging girls in education.
b. Make sure girls and boys are equal in leadership roles during class activities.
c. Favor girls over boys when selecting volunteers in class.
d. Ignore the cultures at home because the culture at school is different.

74. An English language learner (ELL) student from Japan is in a class where the current assignment involves competing with classmates to see who can achieve the highest score in an academic game or contest. Instead of using her high intelligence and competence to defeat classmates, however, she uses it to help them succeed. What is the most likely cultural reason for her behavior?

a. The ELL student, intimidated by being new to the country and school, wants to please peers.
b. The ELL student, being new in the country, school, and class, is trying to make new friends.
c. The ELL student was raised in a culture valuing group cooperation over individual competition.
d. The ELL student feels inferior to classmates due to language barriers and is afraid to compete.

75. Due to chronic underachievement by English language learners, a school has decided to implement a tracking policy in which English language learners are placed into separate, lower-level general classes. What is the most likely outcome of this action?

a. All students in all levels will be held back.
b. English learners will excel because they have more attention given to their needs.
c. The achievement gap between minorities and white Americans will increase.
d. English learners will be less likely to drop out.

76. A third-grade teacher notices that one of her English learners tends to withdraw when she touches his shoulder. What is important for her to consider when she discusses this with his school counselor?

a. There may be physical abuse at home.
b. He may not like her much so doesn't want to be near her.
c. Some cultures do not have high levels of physical contact.
d. He may be scared of her as an authority figure.

77. Describe some cultural differences in how English language learners experience cultural contact in the educational contexts of student interactions and problem-solving and conflict-resolution processes. Describe an instructional approach to address these differences. Explain how this approach would be effective for addressing cultural differences.

78. To apply research findings about how English language learner (ELL) students' school performance is influenced by cultural factors, which of the following teacher practices is MOST appropriate?

a. Teachers respond to ELLs' culturally mediated learning approaches by modifying instruction.
b. Teachers respond to ELL students by emphasizing language instruction over cultural factors.
c. Teachers respond to ELLs by developing comprehensive curricula for US cultural immersion.
d. Teachers respond to cultural factors by grouping ELL students sharing cultural backgrounds.

79. Which of the following is an accurate description of either the internal elements or external elements of a culture?

a. The language of a culture is an internal element.
b. The structures of families are external elements.
c. The gender roles in groups are internal elements.
d. The social roles in cultures are external elements.

80. Regarding the history of education, which statement is MOST accurate?

a. Prior to *Brown v. Board of Education,* classes within schools were racially segregated.
b. Prior to *Brown v. Board of Education,* black students were excluded from white schools.
c. Prior to *Brown v. Board of Education,* schools were legally integrated but remained unequal.
d. Prior to *Brown v. Board of Education,* American schools excluded immigrant students.

Answer Key and Explanations for Test #1

Language Concepts and Language Acquisition

1. D: Morphemes are the smallest units of language that have meaning. For example, "devalue" is made of the morphemes "de," which means opposite or not, and "value," which means something that is important or useful. These cannot be broken down further. Greek and Latin roots are morphemes that help all students understand the meaning of words as well as be able to infer the meanings of words they do not know.

2. C: Cognates are words that have similar meanings and spellings because they come from the same origin. Although false cognates do exist, students can benefit greatly from cognate awareness from as early as preschool. Teachers should teach cognates while also making students aware of false cognates.

3. B: Persuasive writing presents an argument supporting a point of view. Although comparing different types of essays may be helpful, to write a persuasive essay, students need to focus on purpose and structure rather than on vocabulary. Answer D, discussing and writing drafts, should come only after students have a firm understanding of key aspects of persuasive writing.

4. A: Several English phonemes are not found in other languages. The Japanese language does not contain phonemes such as /dʒ/, /th/, and the /schwa/. English learners who come from backgrounds that do not have certain English phonemes may have trouble with hearing and pronouncing these particular sounds. Although beginning-level learners do experience a silent period when learning a new language, intermediate-level language learners should be beyond this point.

5. C: Although students can acquire a language without explicit teaching of syntax, systematic and explicit teaching of syntax structures can expedite learning. Although comparing sentence structures from different languages is useful, it is important to consider the language background of learners. If all learners do not speak Spanish, it should not be the only method of teaching subject–predicate pattern and agreement. Worksheets can be helpful but should be used in moderation and come after explicit and direct teaching.

6. A: Total physical response (TPR) stems from a branch of behavioral theory that connects physical action to language. When teachers use TPR, they model an action while saying the word. Direct teaching and mastery learning also stem from behavioral theory; however, these strategies use rigid steps in which teachers follow a scripted lesson. Open Court is an example of direct teaching and mastery learning. Common Underlying Proficiency (CUP) refers to the idea that the primary language and the second language have shared underlying knowledge that allows competence in the second language. CUP is not a teaching methodology but relates to theories of second-language acquisition. Call and response is a strategy that uses choral replies between the teacher and the class, but it does not include physical actions.

7. A: This type of change in language usage in different contexts refers to register switching, which is a skill related to pragmatics. Pragmatics refers to how language is used in pragmatic or practical ways, such as switching language from casual modes to academic modes when entering classrooms. Informal registers might use phrases like "you know" that are acceptable in spoken language but are not acceptable in academic writing. Morphology refers to the components that make up words, so morphological competence refers to the ability to recognize and manipulate morphemes in words. Phonological competence refers to the production of speech sounds and the ability to manipulate sounds in words. Syntactic competence is understanding of sentence structures and word order.

8. A: Phonology is the study of sound patterns as it relates to language. This teacher's activity focuses on phonemes that are part of the English language but may not be present in other languages. This is often confused with phonetics, which is the study of specific speech sounds without context and does not require prior knowledge. Morphology is the study of the meaning of language units, whereas syntax is focused on sentence structure and formation.

9. B: Communicative competence focuses on the importance of communication in interpersonal relationships to create understanding. This method allows students to produce and understand real language used outside of the classroom. This goes beyond grammar drills and focuses on how to use language appropriately in specific contexts. Activities that focus on communicative competence usually include interaction among students instead of having formal presentations or methods of communication.

10. B: Krashen developed the *affective filter hypothesis* in which he considers emotional factors in learning such as self-esteem, motivation, and anxiety. High levels of anxiety can block language learning, which is what the teacher is concerned about. Although background knowledge of Roman history may also affect the learner's presentation, the question focuses on emotional availability of the student rather than knowledge.

11. C: Using the primary language to support learning has been shown to increase not only content learning but also learning of the English language. Advanced students can explain concepts in the primary language to beginning-level students, ensuring that they continue to grow in the content areas as they learn English. Assimilation is the erasure of a student's home culture, so allowing for home language in the classroom would not promote assimilation.

12. B: Prior knowledge impacts students' English language development. Without the appropriate schema and background knowledge, students may have difficulty learning. Although psychological factors or learning disabilities may be at play, this particular learner is already at a beginning-advanced level, and a learning disability should not be the first conclusion a teacher jumps to when considering reasons for student difficulty. Cultural factors may also impact a student's performance at times; however, in this particular scenario, the student is not speaking in front of peers or showing off knowledge in a public way.

13. D: Instructional conversations are a discourse strategy that act as an alternative to teacher-centered classrooms. Discourse is the study of language that considers language beyond grammar or vocabulary. It focuses on the communicative features of language in a particular context. Worksheets and quizzes would not promote discourse as discourse generally requires interaction whether orally or with a text. Although asking a question and seeking a student response is the typical discourse pattern in the classroom, it is teacher-centered and promotes less student discourse.

14. B: Basic interpersonal communication skills (BICS) is the social language and register that is used in everyday life. Students can become proficient in BICS in 6 months or more. On the other hand, cognitive academic language proficiency (CALP), or formal academic language used in schools and workplaces, often takes much longer to develop. In fact, CALP often takes around 7 to 10 years to develop completely. For this student to be behind in CALP is normal because he has only been in the United States for a year.

15. B: Affective filter is activated when students are stressed, or their self-esteem is lowered. Teachers should create a supportive environment with constructive feedback to help students learn while lowering their affective filters. Having students work together in small groups provides a supportive and low-pressure setting for sharing ideas and receiving feedback. Correcting every mistake is often harmful for English learners at the beginning level as production is more important than precision at that stage. Cold-calling students can also heighten anxiety for students; however, ignoring students completely create an environment in which these learners are not included. Students may perceive this as English learners being less valued in the class.

16. A: The error in the sentence has to do with past and present tenses of verbs. The sentence should read "This morning, I **ate** eggs for breakfast." Some languages do not modify the verb to indicate past tense but instead use separate modifiers or context clues such as "this morning" to indicate tense. Appositives are nouns or phrases that explain or identify another noun. For example, "Marty" is an appositive in the sentence "My fat cat Marty was lounging on the couch." Phrasal verbs are verbs in combination with another word, usually an adverb or a preposition, that are idiomatic expressions. For example, "bring up" and "cut off" are two examples of phrasal verbs.

17. A: Dialects are regional or social varieties of a language that differ in pronunciation, vocabulary, or grammar but are generally mutually intelligible. Hindi and Urdu are treated as separate languages for cultural and historical reasons, although they are mutually intelligible in everyday speech. Chinese "dialects" are often classified that way for historical and political reasons and are not mutually intelligible and are considered separate languages. Common examples of true dialects include differences in language due to region, such as New York City and Los Angeles, or social varieties like African American Vernacular English and Southern United States English.

18. C: Positive language transfer occurs when a student's first-language skills can be used to support learning the second language. This often occurs when languages are similar in structure and vocabulary. For example, an Italian speaker will have an easier time learning Spanish than Japanese due to positive language transfer. Teachers can use positive language transfer not only for language structure and vocabulary but also for skills such as phonemic awareness, knowledge of the reading process, and comprehension strategies.

19. D: Krashen's natural order theory posits that certain grammatical language structures are acquired in a specific order. The example here demonstrates this theory because research has demonstrated that "–ing" verbs are generally acquired before "–s" ending to verbs. Interaction hypothesis emphasizes comprehensible input and the importance of conversational interactions to develop language. Affective filter hypothesis focuses on how a student's level of stress affects learning a language. Pivot grammar focuses on the transition children experience when moving from one- word to two-word utterances.

20. C: Discourse includes the way that people interact and use language. Whereas syntax and morphology look at the sentence and word level of language, discourse looks at language in a broader sense in texts as well as behaviors. In particular, discourse can focus on how speakers take turns or show behaviors around listening and using cues when interacting. Discourse is highly contextual and cultural. Language used in the classroom differs significantly from language used at a soccer game or on the playground.

ESL Instruction and Assessment

21. B: Directed reading–thinking activities help support student independence because they emphasize students setting a goal for reading and making and testing their own predictions.

Directed reading activities and listen–read–discuss are both teacher-centered activities that require the teacher to set a purpose for reading and lead discussions. Explicit teaching is also teacher centered, as the teacher is the one explicitly teaching concepts or ideas. Furthermore, reading aloud does not foster independence as much as silent reading.

22. B: Displaying objectives for language development is a key aspect to Specially Designed Academic Instruction in English (SDAIE) in all subjects. Although modifying texts may be appropriate depending on the students' levels, it is important to adapt the text in a way that makes the language more accessible without simplifying the content. In addition, although figurative language and idioms can be difficult for English learners, it is essential, especially at the early-advanced level to expose students to these concepts and help build their knowledge of idioms. Organizers are often a great way to support students' reading comprehension; however, at the early-advanced level, fill-in-the-blanks assignments may be too easy. Instead, an organizer that provides headings and subheadings with spaces for students to write their own summaries and notes would be more appropriate for this level.

23. D: Extended time is most likely the best accommodation to offer the student. Extended time on assessments is often necessary for English language learners because of the additional time needed to process language. By reducing the word problems to mere calculations, the teacher is changing the nature of the examination and may not be assessing the same skills as in the original examination. In addition, if the student is able to use his or her notes, he or she may not show an understanding of formulas that the teacher is testing.

24. D: Structured English Immersion (SEI) is a separate program from Specially Designed Academic Instruction in English (SDAIE). SEI focuses on teaching only in English along with strategies to increase comprehension. SDAIE, on the other hand, may include a student's primary language for support. There are several key components of SDAIE. Teacher attitude is one aspect of SDAIE. In particular, teachers should be open-minded and willing to reflect and learn. Comprehensibility and interaction are also both essential components of the SDAIE model. Comprehensibility means including strategies that enhance comprehension, and interaction means that students have opportunities to discuss the content and ask questions.

25. D: According to Kame'enui and Simmons (2000), the benchmark group may experience some small difficulties when learning concepts. The strategic group shows performance slightly below the benchmark group, whereas the intensive group is often frequently below performance on assessments. The intensive group may need special education support, whereas the strategic group may need additional support and modified curriculum. Students in the strategic group may need visuals and charts to support their learning. Using class discussion may exclude some students from the conversation. In addition, although videos can be helpful, speakers are often fast paced, making it difficult for English learners to pick up on all concepts being taught.

26. A: Teachers should provide English language learner (ELL) students with feedback that is positive as well as corrective rather than only corrective feedback (B). Teachers' feedback also should be comprehensible, not in vocabulary above their level (C) and not restricted only to the specific subject (D), but rather relevant to their lives to be meaningful to ELL students

27. C: Although many of these tools may support students' learning, the tool that would best support vocabulary development is a page with key terms. Formulas are important, but in developing language, students should have a clear understanding of math terms related to this unit, such as surface area, sphere, and rectangular prism. Visual aids can support students' vocabulary development.

28. A: The foundation K-12 curriculum required by Texas under §74.1, Essential Knowledge and Skills of the Texas Administrative Code, includes social studies, comprising history of Texas, America, and the world; government, geography, and economics. Career education (B), physical education (C), and technology applications (D) are all also required, but as part of an enrichment curriculum rather than a foundation curriculum.

29. C: Every lesson should contain objectives about the content area, language development, and learning strategy. A content objective is focused on the knowledge or skills that is specific to a subject matter such as science or social studies, as is shown by answer choices B and D. A language development objective is focused on English language skills such as "writing in compound sentences" in answer choice A. Learning strategy objectives are focused on metacognitive skills that help a student gain knowledge and skills. What sets learning strategies apart from language or content strategies is that learning strategies can be applied across subject areas. Answer choice C is a learning strategy objective.

30. B: The Texas ELPS require English Language Learners (ELLs) to "acquire both social and academic language proficiency in English." This means they must become proficient in "the English needed to think critically, understand, and learn new concepts, process complex academic material, and interact and communicate in English academic settings." (§74.4, English Language Proficiency Standards, Texas Administrative Code, Chapter 74, Subchapter A) This refers to academic English language (A). They must also become proficient in social English language (C), i.e., "the English needed for daily social interactions." Therefore, choice D is also incorrect.

31. C: The ELPS of the TAC requires school districts to identify the proficiency levels of ELL students in listening to (comprehension), speaking, reading, and writing English. They do not limit this identification to reading and writing (A), listening and speaking (B), or reading, writing, and speaking (D).

32. D: When English learners exhibit difficulties in both the primary language and English, there is possibility for a learning disability as Answer D suggests. It is important for teachers to consider the cultural and language differences that may cause issues for learning instead of jumping to special education referral. Irregular schooling is an external factor teachers should be aware of, as this can lead to difficulties. A student being separated from his or her parents is a considerable disruption that could result in academic difficulties. Students with non-alphabetic language backgrounds may have difficulty with sound–symbol relationships, especially when first learning a language.

33. C: The strategy of planning which standards will be taught over the course of the school year and allocating the amount of time each topic will be taught is known as curriculum mapping. Backwards planning is when lessons are intentionally developed with a specific standard in mind. The assessment aligns closely to the standard being taught, and then the activities that would best support the standard are selected. Differentiation occurs when a teacher considers the needs of the students and incorporates choice into process, product, and content. Holistic assessment refers to evaluating a student globally through multiple data points.

34. B: Formative assessments are meant to guide the teacher in understanding what his students know and do not know after a lesson. This information is then used to inform the teacher about what needs to be reviewed and what students have grasped. Rather than a comprehensive assessment that occurs at the end of the unit, formative assessments occur throughout the unit. Exit slips are a way for students to share what they have missed or need to review to meet the standards. Homework questions and quizzes can be a form of formative assessment, however, are less helpful when done as a quick check at the beginning of class. Teachers need time to review the formative assessments to affect their teaching during the next lesson, which can be difficult to do all at the beginning of the class.

35. B: It is important to consider whether or not students have access to technology not only with English learners but with all students. Not every student has internet access at home, nor do they all have computers or laptops. At the advanced level, students should not be using summary frames for writing. Furthermore, it is important to ensure that students are meeting the objectives and standards required. If the objective of the task is to learn about the branches of government, the teacher should ensure that all students including his English learners meet grade-level standards. If he is interested in including culture and students' backgrounds, he could create an additional activity for the entire class in which students compare different models of government that include those from where his students came. It is important to be mindful of separating English learners from the rest of the class.

36. A: Proficiency tests are assessments that measure the level of a student's language ability across different domains. These types of tests are generally given when a new English learner is enrolled in a school. This type of examination does not require preparation on behalf of the student but is related to understanding the student's needs and placement. On the other hand, achievement tests measure what standards a student has achieved by demonstrating certain knowledge and skills that have been taught. Answer B describes formative versus summative assessments. Answers C and D are incorrect.

37. B: Assigning students to create their own semantic maps of words related to a specific topic most develops their skills for classifying and organizing information. They decide whether certain words, phrases, and themes fit into a given category of vocabulary, and arrange the words visually in ways that make sense. They are not using the semantic maps to tell facts apart from opinions (A), to evaluate how reliable any information is (C), or to predict outcomes of any events (D) relative to the vocabulary words.

38. C: It is important to help students develop skills before, during, and after speaking activities. One strategy is to have students engage in positive self-affirmations after speaking. Taking deep breaths and rehearsing is also a good strategy; however, it should occur before speaking. Answer A is not helpful because it can embarrass the student to give feedback in front of the class. Answer B is teacher directed rather than student directed.

39. D: Textbook examinations are those that are provided by the textbook publisher. They often align closely with the content of the textbook and can be more aligned with the state standards and in this case the advanced placement class objectives. This type of test can cover all of the requirements that students must cover for the course. Unfortunately, it often is rigid and does not allow for students' opinions, backgrounds, and cultures. Answer A describes a portfolio assessment in which students have the opportunity to be assessed on pieces of work rather than on one examination. Although this type of assessment may be easier to grade, that should not be the main consideration for choosing an assessment.

40. C: Of the choices offered, the best way to address English language learner (ELL) student needs when state-issued textbooks are provided for all students is to augment them with L1 translations. Giving ELLs subject-content texts issued for lower grade levels (A) is inappropriate: Though the language in these texts may be at a level more accessible to ELLs, they will not receive grade-level subject content. Condensing or summarizing texts (B) is a less acceptable way to modify textbooks as reducing English language reading at the expense of full text means ELLs will not get the same textbook content and features as other students. Replacing textbooks with visuals and objects (D) to avoid English language reading deprives ELLs of the practice they need to develop their English language reading skills for accessing subject content in English.

41. A: Using technology for the sake of using technology is not a justifiable reason to use a resource, including for English learners. Technology should enhance and support the learning process by giving access and allowing new and innovative creations and ideas. It is important that the content is accurate, relevant, and appeals to a variety of learning modalities.

42. C: Error correction can lead to reduced speech as well as lower self-esteem. Especially at the earlier level of language development, production is more important than accuracy. Teachers should focus on students being able to effectively communicate their ideas over accurate grammar, pronunciation, and semantics. Instead, by creating an encouraging open environment, teachers can support language development through lowering students' affective filters. Moreover, although error correction may damage a relationship between student and teacher, in this scenario, students are giving one another error correction rather than the teacher.

43. A: By incorporating realia from students' cultures, students are able to meaningfully contribute to class conversations and are motivated to learn more about instruments. Moreover, students may have background knowledge that can be shared with the class or feel a sense of connection and belonging, which allows for more openness in discussions. Introducing elements from a student's culture does not delay assimilation or a learner's vocabulary skills. Instead, it engages them and helps support language development.

44. D: Modifying the teacher's speech to support English learners includes actions such as modifying phonics, syntax, semantics, pragmatics, and discourse. This might mean repeating key words and simplifying the sentence structure. Teachers can also modify their language by incorporating the primary language to support understanding; however, research shows that decreased teacher talking time allows for the student to have more talking time.

45. A: Applying strategies to try to understand difficult vocabulary words not only allows learners to develop their English language skills but also improves comprehension. Both considering cognates and morphemes are skills that strong readers use to understand passages. Although an outcome of practicing these skills may be improved test taking skills, that should not be the primary reason for this activity. Moreover, using cognates should not be for simply trying to determine which words are true and false cognates but to aid comprehension.

46. B: When considering scaffolding, teachers should first begin with modeling the task that they would like students to be able to accomplish independently. Students observe how the teacher completes the task. The next step is to then have the teacher complete the task with student input, with the teacher primarily completing the task. After that, teachers release responsibility to the students with guided support. Finally, the teacher allows the students to complete the task independently.

47. A: Content focuses on the particular information that is included in the standards for that particular subject. The other three domains—organization, delivery, and fluency—all relate to language-area skills. These include speaking skills such as clear pronunciation, accurate use of grammar, and vocabulary. It also includes pragmatic skills such as use of eye contact and appropriate nonverbal communication with the audience. Organization focuses on the coherence and flow of the information given, which can relate to discourse and semantics.

48. C: At the beginning level, especially for kindergarten, students may not have the capacity to read and write. Instead, students should be asked to show comprehension through realia and illustrations. This might include putting in order pictures that are told in the recording or selecting the picture that accurately represents what was said in the recording. Sentences and written language are not appropriate for this grade level and language development level.

49. B: The Task-Based Language Teaching (TBLT) approach uses real-life examples and tasks to teach language. When teaching about money, the TBLT approach should consider how money is used in the real world and emulate scenarios in which students will use money, such as buying and selling products. Several of these activities can be helpful in developing money sense; however, they do not use the TBLT approach. Bringing in actual money may be inclusive of different cultures and focus on realia, but beyond actual objects, TBLT focuses on scenarios and situations.

50. D: Curriculum calibration refers to determining if a lesson aligns with the standards and in this particular scenario, with English Language Development (ELD) standards. Every lesson should consist of both the content area standards as well as language standards, so curriculum calibration doesn't seek to see if there is a standard connected to the lesson but how well the lesson covers the standard. This may or may not include Specially Designed Academic Instruction in English (SDAIE) strategies, but SDAIE is not required.

51. B: Involving communities and families in the school increases student achievement because students feel that the school culture and home culture may create less dissonance. The message sent by the school by doing this is that their home culture is accepted and celebrated in this educational space. Although this format can provide opportunities for students to ask questions, it mainly bridges the connection between school and home. Depending on the language proficiency of the speaker, these talks may support language acquisition; however, that is not a primary goal.

52. Essay question graders commonly look for the following elements in a strong response: strong content knowledge, clear organization, and effective arguments or examples. Language and usage are not usually strictly graded, but they can make a big impact on the clarity of your ideas.

Please use the provided rubric to make sure your response meets these common criteria. Try to have a friend or family member grade your response for you or take a break after writing your response and return to grade it with fresh eyes.

Constructed Response Rubric

Domain	Description
Content Knowledge	• The response directly addresses every part of the prompt. • The response demonstrates independent knowledge of the topic. • The response discusses the topic at an appropriate depth.
Organization	• The response introduces the topic, usually with a thesis statement or by restating the prompt. • The response directly addresses the prompt by providing a clear and concise answer or solution. • The answer or solution is supported by logical arguments or evidence. • The response restates the main idea in the conclusion.
Arguments and Examples	• The response provides a reasonable answer to the prompt. • The answer is supported by strong reasoning or evidence. • The response develops ideas logically and connects ideas to one another. • The reasoning and evidence provided act to support a unified main idea.
Language and Usage	• The response demonstrates effective use of grammar and uses varied sentence structure throughout the response. • The response demonstrates correct use of spelling, punctuation, and capitalization. • The response demonstrates strong and varied use of vocabulary relevant to the topic and appropriate for the intended audience.

53. Essay question graders commonly look for the following elements in a strong response: strong content knowledge, clear organization, and effective arguments or examples. Language and usage are not usually strictly graded, but they can make a big impact on the clarity of your ideas.

Please use the provided rubric to make sure your response meets these common criteria. Try to have a friend or family member grade your response for you or take a break after writing your response and return to grade it with fresh eyes.

Constructed Response Rubric

Domain	Description
Content Knowledge	• The response directly addresses every part of the prompt. • The response demonstrates independent knowledge of the topic. • The response discusses the topic at an appropriate depth.
Organization	• The response introduces the topic, usually with a thesis statement or by restating the prompt. • The response directly addresses the prompt by providing a clear and concise answer or solution. • The answer or solution is supported by logical arguments or evidence. • The response restates the main idea in the conclusion.
Arguments and Examples	• The response provides a reasonable answer to the prompt. • The answer is supported by strong reasoning or evidence. • The response develops ideas logically and connects ideas to one another. • The reasoning and evidence provided act to support a unified main idea.
Language and Usage	• The response demonstrates effective use of grammar and uses varied sentence structure throughout the response. • The response demonstrates correct use of spelling, punctuation, and capitalization. • The response demonstrates strong and varied use of vocabulary relevant to the topic and appropriate for the intended audience.

54. A: Role, audience, format, topic (RAFT) is a post-reading strategy that can be applied flexibly to support students in responding in writing to reflect about and analyze their reading. The teacher or class makes suggestions from which students select a role to play, an audience to address, a format to use, and a topic to cover in writing about what they have read. The question-answer relationships (QAR) (B) strategy is used before, during, and after reading to help students identify the four question-answer relationships most common in the texts they will read—"Right There," "Think and Search," "Author and You," and "On My Own" questions—and answer these about the text. Questions only (C) is used before, during, and after reading as a strategy to teach students how to ask questions about the text and read actively to answer them. The reader's-writer's notebook (D) is a strategy used before, during, and after reading for students to have conversations with and about text, connecting their own thoughts, background, prior knowledge, opinions, and biases to the reading to build comprehension.

55. A: English language learners (ELLs) with intermediate English language proficiency (ELP) can be impeded seriously in learning subject content by unfamiliar, content-specific language structures and vocabulary, particularly equation and formula syntax and technical terminology in mathematics and science subjects. When planning Specially Designed Academic Instruction in English (SDAIE) for middle school ELLs at the intermediate level of ELP, the teacher can give them better access to algebra content by integrating language objectives for these specialized elements into every lesson. Restricting instruction to skills and concepts at lower developmental levels (B) is inappropriate, as these do not match the students' developmental levels, regardless of their ELP levels. Putting off advanced lessons until ELLs reach advanced receptive ELP (C) is both inappropriate and unrealistic, as this could take too long for them to learn algebra at the right time; plus, individual student ELPs progress at varying rates. Lesson planning to avoid language just because math uses it less than other subjects (D) is also inappropriate for teaching SDAIE, which should still incorporate English language while emphasizing content learning, as its name indicates.

56. B: By visibly placing and making regular use of content-related objects like maps, artifacts, prints, and puzzles, teachers provide stimuli to start conversations with and among students. By arranging the physical classroom space so students are accessible to each other (A), teachers establish a physical setting that supports student interactions in general—conversations, study collaborations, and other interactions. By displaying and using various printed materials in both English and the students' native languages (C), teachers provide students with a language-rich environment. Because each of these has the related but distinct specific effects described, using all of these classroom techniques equally (D) is incorrect.

Foundations of ESL Education, Cultural Awareness, and Family and Community Involvement

57. C: An appropriate intercultural communication strategy is to find out which terms are acceptable and unacceptable to certain cultural groups and then to use the acceptable terms to describe them. If others use unacceptable terms to describe them, members of all cultural groups should say so and say what they want to be called. Rather than substituting Americanized names, which does not make newcomers feel welcome (A), it is important to learn the correct spelling, pronunciation, and sequence of the names that others want to be called and any applicable titles showing respect. Another strategy is to avoid applying generalizations about cultural groups to individuals from those groups (B). Rather than maintaining your usual interpersonal space (D), it is better to observe the space people from other cultures use when determining the appropriate distance. Standing too close to or far from people from other cultures can cause them great discomfort.

58. A: Social distance is the perceived separation between individuals based on social groups such as gender, ethnicity, and language. Social distance can create prejudice and bias in individuals. To reduce social distance, teachers can foster relationships among diverse students as well as highlight the value of multicultural education. What the teacher has done is actually support multicultural perspectives and cultural relativism. Cultural relativism is the idea that all thoughts, words, and actions exist in a cultural context. With more perspectives added, one's cultural relativism increases. Acculturation is the adaptation to another dominant culture. These activities could increase acculturation if individuals from the dominant culture are involved.

59. D: Although refreshments can be a nice touch, they are not an essential part of parent–teacher conferences. It is important for schools and teachers to consider having an interpreter if parents do not speak English. Moreover, there may be cultural differences in perceptions of time as well as of involvement in schools. It is important to communicate these expectations and create alternatives to allow for these cultural differences. Furthermore, some families may be working during the school day, making it difficult for parents to come to school during that time. This doesn't apply to only English learners but all learners.

60. C: According to Pew research conducted in 2023, Mexico is the largest source country of immigrants in the U.S. (about 10.9 million). The second-largest immigrant population comes from India (about 2.9 million). By comparison, China is about 2.4 million and the Philippines is about 2.1 million.

61. D: Cultural relativism is the idea that all thoughts, words, and actions exist in a cultural context. On the other hand, ethnocentrism is the idea that one's culture and cultural values are the norm. In this perspective, individuals are unable to understand other cultural values and beliefs. Ethical relativism is similar, but it is the belief that morals and values are all formed in accordance with societal, cultural, and individual perspectives and experiences. Cultural pluralism is the idea that there are many different cultures within a society or country.

62. B: Changing the teacher's level of physical contact based on the student's perceived comfort levels and cultural norms would not be wise for the teacher to do so because it can be construed as favoring certain students over others. Furthermore, it can confuse students as to what the norm is around physical contact between a figure of authority such as the teacher and the student. Maintaining clear and consistent expectations and behaviors helps students learn what the norm is for the school's culture.

63. C: Cultural concepts about time differ across different countries and cultures. Some cultures such as the United States value strict organization around time as well as efficiency and speed. Intelligence is often associated with speed in the American context. Other cultures, however, may not value time in the same way. It is important for teachers to be aware of their own time values and work within the school structure to support the student. This means that they may not be able to completely change the schedule or force the student to speed up.

64. D: According to Morey and Kitano (1997), there are three levels of incorporating diversity. The first level is exclusive, which includes more surface-level and stereotypical depictions of culture. These are elements of cultures such as the food, the dress, and the games associated with a culture. Inclusive is the enhancement of the curriculum through adding diverse perspectives; however, it often holds the same central structure at the original curriculum. Transformed curriculum is built on completely new perspectives and is developed with a completely different structure. Additive refers to Banks' model on multicultural education, which is similar to the inclusive level.

65. C: Cooperative learning groups foster higher levels of interaction among students, which provides a classroom that supports diverse learning environments and is inclusive. Although conflicts may occur, with proper support, students will be able to overcome issues and work together. Semantic skills deal with understanding the meaning of language. Cooperative groups do not necessarily enhance semantic skills, although it might support better communication skills. Finally, it won't necessarily divide the class unless competition among groups is a prominent part of the class structure.

66. D: Biculturalism is a term used to describe individuals who are able to fully function within two different cultures without having to reject either culture. Individuals who are bicultural often are able to connect with their primary culture and that of the dominant culture. Answer A describes an individual who is perhaps acculturated but still is more comfortable in his primary culture and language. Answer B describes an individual experiencing assimilation, and Answer C is someone who has rejected the dominant culture.

67. B: Various cultures have differences in their written discourse. In America, features of written academic language tend to be distant, authoritative, concise, and clear. In other cultures, discourse may focus on storytelling and being less direct. Language is not only a reflection of knowledge but also culture, so it is important for teachers to take this into consideration as they teach and grade writing. Although it is important to explicitly teach the expectations of academic writing in the American setting, it is important to also allow flexibility and types of writing activities that build on students' cultures.

68. B: Simply including diverse literature in the curriculum is not enough to create an inclusive environment. Many "diverse" books can include stereotypical depictions of minority characters, including women. Although having multiple translations can be helpful, it is not essential when thinking about what texts to choose to teach. Well-known authors may be beneficial as it can draw the interest of students, but it is not required, and considering the author for a talk at the school depends on the funding available, which may not always be possible.

69. C: There are a multitude of reasons that may be an explanation for why the parents are not involved. These might include different values around family involvement in education. Some cultures do not have heavy family involvement in schooling due to a number of reasons such as respect toward the teacher. Lack of involvement, however, should not be confused with cultural deprivation or disinterest in education. On the contrary, many families have reported that they are supportive of their children's education. Moreover, although parental education has an impact, it does not mean that they are illiterate, especially because the student is in second grade.

70. A: The model minority myth is the destructive belief that Asian Americans all excel in academic areas, especially math and science. This myth is dangerous in that it can lead the teacher to believe that the student does not have any problems. The teacher's stereotype that Asian students should excel in math may cause her to misinterpret normal academic struggle as a disability rather than considering other factors. When self-reflecting, teachers should consider factors such as if other students are also struggling, which could indicate that they have not taught the content in a way that is accessible to all students. The teacher should also consider the language level of the student. In this case, the student is at the advanced level, so it is possible that the student is not experiencing culture shock nor has a language barrier that is causing these difficulties.

71. B: Several schools have added negotiation and mediation courses for students that have proven effective in reducing violence and vandalism as well as improving race relations. It is important that schools consider holistically a variety of strategies to implement rather than going with a single solution. Simply placing diverse students in the same classes alone does not improve cultural communication, and making disciplinary measures more stringent may actually have a negative effect.

72. A: Naming interviews are seen as an activity that helps affirm students' identities because names are often deeply rooted in culture. Names hold value within a culture and are associated with certain meanings. By allowing students to discuss this in the classroom, students are able to bring an important aspect of themselves—their names—to light. Although show and tell can be culturally affirming, it doesn't necessarily have to do with a student's cultural identity. Activities that validate students' cultural identities should focus on the student.

73. B: One possible cultural difference between America and other countries includes gender difference regarding academic achievement and education. Some cultures do not stress academic achievement for women. To equitably support girls in classrooms, it is important to try to foster leadership skills equally in both girls and boys in the class. Neglecting one gender can lead to an imbalance and can send a strong message to the class. Rather than being confrontational, approaching parents with an open mind and respecting cultural differences are key to fostering good relationships with families.

74. C: This student was raised in a collectivist culture typical of many Asian, Latin American, and other countries. American culture is individualistic, valuing competition and individual expression; collectivist cultures value cooperation above competition, often disapprove of individual expression outside of cultural norms, and advocate deferring one's own needs for the sake of group harmony and furthering the common good. Whereas the individual is paramount in the United States, in collectivist cultures, the group takes precedence. Rather than being intimidated, wanting to please her peers (A), trying to make new friends (B), or feeling inferior and afraid to compete (D) as motives, the most likely cultural reason for this student's behavior is to conform to the values of her native culture.

75. C: Tracking has been shown to increase the achievement gap between minorities and white Americans. Although many people argue the efficient and realistic response that tracking provides, it can lead to lower expectations, which could lead to dropping out. Moreover, although some groups of students may be held back, such as those placed in generalized and less academic tracks, others may excel. This does not justify the benefits of tracking because not all students benefit.

76. C: Physical contact and distance between speakers is highly cultural. Some cultures use frequent physical contact when talking with one another, whereas other cultures maintain distance and feel awkward or embarrassed when physical contact occurs. It is important to keep this in mind when dealing with students from different cultural backgrounds. This behavior from the student may not necessarily mean that there is physical abuse occurring at home or that the speaker has any particular feelings toward the teacher.

77. Essay question graders commonly look for the following elements in a strong response: strong content knowledge, clear organization, and effective arguments or examples. Language and usage are not usually strictly graded, but they can make a big impact on the clarity of your ideas.

Please use the provided rubric to make sure your response meets these common criteria. Try to have a friend or family member grade your response for you or take a break after writing your response and return to grade it with fresh eyes.

Constructed Response Rubric

Domain	Description
Content Knowledge	• The response directly addresses every part of the prompt. • The response demonstrates independent knowledge of the topic. • The response discusses the topic at an appropriate depth.
Organization	• The response introduces the topic, usually with a thesis statement or by restating the prompt. • The response directly addresses the prompt by providing a clear and concise answer or solution. • The answer or solution is supported by logical arguments or evidence. • The response restates the main idea in the conclusion.
Arguments and Examples	• The response provides a reasonable answer to the prompt. • The answer is supported by strong reasoning or evidence. • The response develops ideas logically and connects ideas to one another. • The reasoning and evidence provided act to support a unified main idea.
Language and Usage	• The response demonstrates effective use of grammar and uses varied sentence structure throughout the response. • The response demonstrates correct use of spelling, punctuation, and capitalization. • The response demonstrates strong and varied use of vocabulary relevant to the topic and appropriate for the intended audience.

78. A: Research studies find many English language learner (ELL) students perform below their abilities academically. Investigators believe cultural disparities between school and home contribute to these achievement gaps. They recommend teachers address diverse learning approaches through culturally responsive instruction as a solution rather than concentrating on language at the expense of culture (B), attempting to change ELL students culturally through curricula (C), or homogeneously grouping ELL students according to their cultural backgrounds (D).

79. C: Internal elements of a culture are the parts that are not visible and generally revolve around what people in a culture believe and value. External elements are the visible or observable aspects, which include many elements. Gender roles, beliefs, values, mores, customs, worldviews, expectations, rituals and rites, nonverbal communication patterns, and work and leisure patterns are examples of internal elements of cultures. Family structures (B) also are examples of internal cultural elements, as are social roles (D) and status. Languages (A) are external, not internal elements of cultures, as are religious structures, governments, and technology; arts and literature; and food, shelter, and clothing.

80. B: Before the 1954 US Supreme Court decision in *Brown v. Board of Education*, in many states, especially in the South, public schools were racially segregated by law into separate all-white and all-black schools; within those segregated schools, individual classes were not further divided by race. (A). The basis of this landmark lawsuit was that black students were prohibited from attending white schools. Black schools were deemed "separate but equal." In *Brown v. Board of*

Education, the Supreme Court ruled that segregated education was inherently unequal, overturning the antiquated "separate but equal" provision of *Plessy v. Ferguson* (1896). Prior to *Brown v Board of Education*, schools were legally segregated (C). In the early 1950s, white schools did not exclude white immigrant students (D) the same way they excluded black American students.

Practice Test #2

Language Concepts and Language Acquisition

Refer to the following for questions 1–2:

Since coming to America, a student from Italy, Fredo, has learned to speak English using different vocabulary and phrasing when addressing his teachers than he uses when conversing with his friends. He shows strengths in oral communication, including good eye contact and expressive physical gestures. However, his American classmates are put off by his maintaining closer physical proximity than they expect when conversing with them.

1. Fredo speaking in a different manner to his teachers and friends is an example of which of the following?

a. The influence of contextual discourse factors on language variation choices
b. The persistence of a native regional dialect's characteristics after relocating
c. The differences between English language learner (ELL) students' correct and incorrect constructions
d. The influence of an ELL student's native language on his speaking in English

2. Fredo's cultural difference in body language a feature of which of the following?

a. Discourse in using language
b. Semantics in using language
c. Pragmatics in using language
d. Social functions of language

3. Sylvia is a high school English language learner (ELL). When given oral discourse activities, she is very good at addressing points classmates have just brought up, organizing her ideas, unifying her overall message, and finding appropriate English words and phrases to make connections and transitions between sentences; however, she speaks very slowly, with many pauses and interruptions between phrases and sentences. On which area does she need to work?

a. Responsiveness
b. Coherence
c. Cohesion
d. Fluency

4. A high school teacher wants to familiarize ELL students with standard discourse structures and conventions used in academic essays. Which activity would be most appropriate for this purpose?

a. Assign small groups to brainstorm essay topics, write short drafts, and analyze these together.
b. Give them copies of essays with key vocabulary words missing, and have them complete these.
c. Have them analyze various essay types, and identify which vocabulary and grammar they share.
d. Help them analyze provided sample essays, and make graphic organizers of various essay types.

5. Which of the following is a morphological feature?

a. The combination of roots and affixes
b. The patterns of intonation in speech
c. The pitches of a voice during speech
d. The relationship of letters to sounds

6. Which of the following English words has a Greek origin?

a. Calorie
b. Calendar
c. Calumny
d. Calisthenics

7. Of the following words, which has roots in both Greek and Latin?

a. Index
b. Calcium
c. Campus
d. Candle

8. Among the following pairs, which two words share the same Latin or Greek source word??

a. Clinic and recline
b. Clause and clavicle
c. Clavicle and clavichord
d. Iconoclast and claustrophobia

9. To promote English learners' language development, what does knowledge of morphology informing word analysis related to *solve, solvent, solution; absolve, absolute, absolution;* and *dissolve, dissolute, dissolution* most promote?

a. Spelling
b. Fluency
c. Vocabulary
d. None of these

10. Why might Spanish-speaking English language learner (ELL) students fail to pronounce the initial letter *h* in English words?

a. There is no such letter in their native language alphabet.
b. There are no similar phonemes in their native language.
c. The letter *h* is always silent when it is the initial letter in Spanish.
d. They are generalizing from some English silent-h words.

11. If an ELL is at the Intermediate level described by the Texas ELPS for Listening, the teacher needs to design and use instruction including "extensive linguistic supports and adaptations such as visuals, slower speech and other verbal cues, simplified language, gestures, and preteaching to preview or build topic-related vocabulary":

a. When the conversation topic is unfamiliar
b. Even when a conversation topic is familiar
c. Only sometimes to support understanding
d. With highly specialized/complex language

12. An English language learner (ELL) student writes this sentence: "Understanding spoken English and speaking in English is harder for me than reading and writing English." What is the error in this sentence?

a. The word order
b. The tense of the verb
c. Subject–verb agreement
d. None of these

13. An elementary English language learner (ELL) student has learned some English expressions from American classmates and demonstrates his learning by greeting the school principal, "Hey, man! What's up?" This child has not yet mastered which feature of pragmatics?

a. Idiom
b. Setting
c. Register
d. Purpose

14. English language learner (ELL) Jose's teacher helps him build his English vocabulary by pointing out and listing Spanish–English cognates, showing him their identical or similar spelling and modeling and explaining their differences in pronunciation. What is this instructional strategy mostly an example of?

a. Using the student's prior L1 knowledge
b. Teaching students decoding skills
c. Systematic instruction in phonics
d. Applying word analysis methods

15. Which of the following examples reflects a geographic influence on language variation?

a. The politically separated parts of a city or country, for example, Berlin and Korea, developed different usages.
b. A village isolated in a mountain valley retained Elizabethan English forms for centuries.
c. Some African Americans use nonstandard English with unique idiomatic expressions.
d. Some low-income families lacking formal education use ungrammatical constructions.

16. Regarding coherence and cohesion in written and oral discourse, which of these is true?

a. Coherence and cohesion are different words with the same meanings.
b. Coherence is an overall unity of organization; cohesion is more specific.
c. Coherence involves connecting sentences; cohesion involves topic sentences.
d. Coherence uses pronouns and repetition; cohesion involves thesis statements.

17. A female student from an Asian country habitually avoids eye contact when interacting with teachers and school administrators. How can school personnel best address her pragmatic needs to develop her sociolinguistic competence?

a. Refuse to interact unless she makes eye contact to eliminate the old behavior and reward a new one.
b. Acknowledge her cultural norm, and make her comfortable by avoiding all eye contact in interactions.
c. Explain the importance of eye contact in the United States, and assign her to research and write an essay on it.
d. Respect her cultural norm, make new norms explicit, and gently encourage eye contact without forcing it.

18. Which type of theory most attributes language acquisition to the influences of context, world knowledge, and motivation to achieve goals?

a. Social interactionist theory
b. Behaviorist theory
c. Cognitive theory
d. Nativist theory

19. According to cognitive developmental theory related to language acquisition, learning and discussing definitions of vocabulary words like *free will, truth, beauty*, and *love* would be most developmentally appropriate for which age or grade levels?

a. PreK to grade 2
b. Grades 3 to 5
c. Grades 6 to 8
d. Grades 9 to 12

ESL Instruction and Assessment

20. To instruct English language learner (ELL) students in a cross-disciplinary unit that integrates math and English language development (ELD), which of the following approaches would be MOST effective?

a. Using peer tutoring
b. Using team teaching
c. Using educational technologies
d. Using bilingual paraprofessionals

21. For English language learner (ELL) students in kindergarten through Grade 1, which of the following strategies to scaffold tasks requiring academic language proficiency would be LEAST developmentally appropriate?

a. Realia
b. Analogies
c. Manipulatives
d. None of these would be developmentally appropriate.

22. A teacher of English language learners (ELLs) wants to modify the language in a learning exercise without simplifying it. Which of the following would best help the teacher accomplish this?

a. Repeat utterances.
b. Use easier word choices.
c. Speak or read aloud slower.
d. Exaggerate syllables or use word stress.

23. The last sentence of a story has this line of dialogue, spoken between two married adults: "Come on, honey; let's go home." A student reading or hearing this story would demonstrate the inferential level of meaning by which of the following responses?

a. The couple went home together.
b. The story had a happy ending for them.
c. The author wanted a happy end for readers.
d. The readers will be more satisfied by this end.

24. A teacher with a mainstream English language classroom that includes English language learner (ELL) students as well as native English-speaking students always calls on the first student to raise a hand after he or she asks the class a question. An administrator observes the class and finds the ELL students never get to answer, although some of them do raise their hands. What instructional practice does the teacher need to change?

a. Provide enough wait time.
b. Frame questions appropriately.
c. Vary the question types by need.
d. Do all of these.

25. A Spanish-speaking English language learner (ELL) student has early-advanced English language proficiency (ELP) and good literacy in her L1 but never received formal instruction in grammar constructions or terminology in her home country. Encountering an English-language textbook assignment requiring a conditional-subjunctive sentence construction, she asks the teacher what this means. Using the cognates, *condicional* and *subjuntivo,* is not helpful. Instead, the teacher gives the student an example of a conditional-subjunctive sentence in Spanish. Upon reading it, the student understands what kind of sentence is needed for the English-language assignment. What kind of learning strategy has the teacher used?

a. Metacognitive
b. Metalinguistic
c. Vocabulary
d. Translation

26. When reading an English text, an English language learner (ELL) student recalls that the phrase *jump the gun* used in the text is an idiom meaning to take an action or draw a conclusion prematurely. The student has accessed which type of memory?

a. Declarative memory
b. Procedural memory
c. Episodic memory
d. All of these

27. A teacher provides kindergarten English language learner (ELL) students with artifacts, clothes, and other real objects from the students' native countries. The teacher also teaches the whole class the names and uses of these objects. What is this most apt to accomplish?

a. Further students' understanding of US challenges to various immigrant groups.
b. Interfere with students' acculturation to the United States by using objects from other cultures.
c. Interfere with students' English language development (ELD) in vocabulary by teaching them words from other languages.
d. Further students' ELD by stimulating conversations through interaction with known objects.

28. A first-grade teacher has a tradition of telling students a story every year that includes a Thanksgiving celebration. This year, he has some English language learner (ELL) students from other countries for the first time. How can he best adapt his practice to include them?

a. Eliminate the tradition and simply stop telling the story.
b. Incorporate a holiday that some ELL students observe.
c. Modify the story with a more universal family occasion.
d. Continue the tradition, so ELLs learn the United States' culture.

29. A teacher has a class of English language learner (ELL) students. One group of these students never had any formal education in their home countries; the other group did. The teacher differentiates instruction to meet their differing ______ needs.

a. cultural
b. linguistic
c. cognitive
d. academic

30. Which of the following is a software program that would most benefit an English language learner (ELL) student for learning to speak English like a native?

a. The English as a second language (ESL Jobs Forum)
b. The Reading Plus system
c. Rosetta Stone's software
d. Software For Students' Easy Writer

31. For fifth-grade English language learner (ELL) students who are at the intermediate English language proficiency (ELP) level, a teacher needs to select printed instructional materials to use in a lesson about rock formation. Which of the following is the most appropriate way for the teacher to guide material selection?

a. Choosing a fifth-grade text and adapting its syntax and vocabulary
b. Substituting manipulatives and graphics for printed text materials
c. Substituting a concise outline of key subject facts instead of texts
d. Choosing a fourth- or third-grade text to match student ELP levels

32. One theoretical basis for recent (2014) English language learner (ELL) literacy approaches is the interactive reading model. Which of the following is true of this model?

a. It emphasizes interpretation skills rather than decoding skills.
b. It regards reading as proceeding from the parts to the whole.
c. It regards reading as proceeding from the whole to the parts.
d. It emphasizes that reading can proceed from the parts to the whole or from the whole to the parts.

33. Recent studies find that, relative to English language and literacy development for adolescent English language learner (ELL) students who are refugees with little, interrupted, or no formal education, teaching early reading strategies:

a. is ineffective, as it is developmentally inappropriate for their age levels
b. often enables them to advance by eight reading levels in one semester
c. enhances their reading fluency but does not improve their vocabularies
d. is not applicable because they have age-level print literacy skills in their L1s

34. According to the Texas ELPS, what is the ability of ELL students at the Advanced level for writing in English for participation in grade-level/grade-appropriate shared writing activities?

a. They cannot participate meaningfully in any grade-appropriate shared English writing activities.
b. They can participate meaningfully only on familiar, concrete topics using high-frequency English.
c. They can participate meaningfully in most grade-level shared writing activities with SLA support.
d. They can participate meaningfully in most grade-appropriate shared writing activities in English.

35. An English language learner (ELL) student reads a text on world history that lists events in chronological order beginning with the assassination of Archduke Ferdinand. The student comments that this assassination triggered a series of occurrences that culminated in World War I. Which process of reading comprehension has this student MOST demonstrated?

a. Making inferences from reading text
b. Identifying facts and opinions in text
c. Identifying cause and effect in a text
d. Relating one's experiences to a text

36. An English language learner (ELL) student has written a composition. Pursuant to teacher feedback, the student adds certain words and phrases to make clearer, more logical connections between some sentences and paragraphs and removes some language that adds words but not meaning. Which writing aspect of the writing process does this demonstrate?

a. Organization
b. Evaluation
c. Revision
d. Focus

37. An English language learner (ELL) student writes, "I just visited Washington dc for the frist time." In which English language convention does this sentence NOT contain an error?

a. Spelling
b. Grammar
c. Punctuation
d. Capitalization

38. When a teacher makes a lesson plan using Specially Designed Academic Instruction in English (SDAIE), which must he or she include?

a. Learning objectives for English language literacy
b. Learning objectives for academic English language
c. Learning objectives for grade-level subject content
d. Learning objectives for all of these

39. An English language learner (ELL) high school student had limited formal education and literacy in his L1, but he can relate personally to a school text about water wells because he had experience building wells in a refugee camp before coming to the United States. How can the teacher take advantage of this?

a. Scaffolding student interactions with the text
b. Accessing the student's previous knowledge
c. Scaffolding the teacher–student interactions
d. Strategies to create background knowledge

40. Among the following contextual supports, which would be MOST cognitively engaging for English language learner (ELL) students in Grades prekindergarten, kindergarten, and 1?

a. Realia
b. Manipulatives
c. Focus questions
d. A and B

41. A teacher is planning a Specially Designed Academic Instruction in English (SDAIE) lesson to teach social studies content to English language learner (ELL) students and wants to promote their active use of language regarding the content they will be learning. Which of the following is FALSE about this lesson?

a. The teacher should not let students use their L1s as it will interfere with their L2.
b. The teacher can assign cooperative learning tasks to promote active language use.
c. The teacher can facilitate active language use by allowing students to use their L1s.
d. The teacher should add contextual aids into the social studies content to make it more comprehensible.

42. Which of the following assignments incorporates all four Cs of creativity, critical thinking, collaboration, and communication throughout the entire activity?

a. Having students independently plan and then execute their own projects to solve problems
b. Having students in small groups plan problem-solving projects and execute them independently
c. Having students in small groups plan and execute original problem-solving projects as a joint effort
d. Having students independently plan and then execute original problem-solving projects together

43. When teaching English language learners (ELLs), which of the following would be the MOST effective scaffolding strategy for accessing prior knowledge to introduce new concepts and vocabulary words in English?

a. Relate concepts and words to culturally familiar ideas and L1 words in comparison.
b. Compare concepts to similar new ideas, and offer multiple English word synonyms.
c. Provide multiple visual aids illustrating new concepts and English vocabulary words.
d. Design a hands-on learning activity wherein students use new concepts and words.

44. Which of the following is the best example of a teacher question during a Specially Designed Academic Instruction in English (SDAIE) chemistry lesson to promote critical thinking skills?

a. What are the names of all seven of the noble gases?
b. Of the gases we discussed, which ones are noble?
c. Which of the gases we discussed are inert gases?
d. Is it easy or hard to compound noble gases? Why?

45. Of the following statements, which is accurate regarding front-loading vocabulary for English language learners (ELLs)?

a. Before assigning reading, teachers must first scan the text to identify problematic vocabulary.
b. For comprehension, students need a working knowledge of 75% of the vocabulary in the text.
c. Identifying their students' Lexile levels will not help teachers for front-loading text vocabulary.
d. Identifying student Lexile levels is useful, but Lexile Analyzer does not help with specific texts.

46. A teacher instructs English language learner (ELL) students in different text genres. After they have demonstrated the ability to identify text samples correctly by genre, the teacher provides each student with text in one genre and gives them an assignment to transform it into another genre. What research evidence supports this instructional practice?

a. None; the teacher is simply giving the students English writing practice.
b. Explicit instruction in genres promotes improvement in ELL writing skills.
c. Having students switch among genres does not help them focus on text.
d. This instructional practice benefits ELLs but not native English speakers.

47. A teacher preparing Specially Designed Academic Instruction in English (SDAIE) lessons for English language learner (ELL) students mainstreamed in an English-language class is planning small-group collaborative work to discuss their analyses and interpretations of English literature texts. What is the best way to group students for this assignment?

a. The ELL students should be grouped homogeneously to facilitate communication.
b. The ELL and native English-speaking students should be grouped heterogeneously.
c. The ELL students should be grouped heterogeneously but at least two per group.
d. The ELL and native English-speaking students' grouping will not make a difference.

48. Among long-term ELs, under-schooled ELs, and Generation 1.5 ELs, which populations are more likely to have spent the same amount of time in the United States education system by the time they are high school seniors?

a. Long-term ELs and Generation 1.5 ELs
b. Long-term ELs and under-schooled ELs
c. Undereducated and Generation 1.5 ELs
d. All three of these

49. Which of these is the MOST appropriate use of a summative assessment?

a. Determining at the end of a unit if students achieved state standards on which instruction is based
b. Determining during instruction whether students are making sufficient progress to meet standards
c. Determining how to modify ongoing instruction so it will more effectively address students' needs
d. Determining how to design further differentiated, standards-based instruction for given students

50. If grade-appropriate stories are read aloud in English to ELL students at the Beginning level for reading English described by the Texas ELPS, they can obtain appreciable meaning from them if:

a. The stories include low frequency, abstract, unpracticed English.
b. They are not distracted by illustrations, gestures, objects, or mime.
c. They are not distracted by slow speech and careful enunciation.
d. The stories are read aloud to them in short "chunks"/segments.

51. How does Wiggins and McTighe's Backward Design differ from other instructional planning processes?

a. Teachers have to plan a range of assessments before planning learning experiences.
b. Teachers have to plan learning experiences and a range of assessments concurrently.
c. Teachers have to replace traditional assessments with authentic performance tasks.
d. Teachers have to plan learning experiences first and assessments at the end of units.

52. An English language test gets very similar results across repeated administrations to native English-speaking students but widely varying results when administered repeatedly to English language learner (ELL) students. What is this assessment issue MOST related to?

a. Validity
b. Reliability
c. Test bias
d. Administration procedure

53. A class including both native English-speaking and English language learner (ELL) students is given an English language arts (ELA) test. All of the ELL students score greater than two standard deviations below all of the native English-speaking students. Analyzing the item scores, teachers discover the ELL students performed at grade level in all English language development (ELD) areas—vocabulary words, grammar, fluency, and so on, but the test contained an excessive number of idiomatic expressions unfamiliar to them. Which statement best represents this assessment issue?

a. This test was biased by too much content ELLs could not be expected to know.
b. This test was unreliable because ELLs scored much lower than native students.
c. This test was invalid because the ELLs scored greater than two standard deviations below the other students.
d. This test was unbiased, reliable, and valid and revealed a weakness of the ELLs.

54. Which of the following is a strategy important to use in Specially Designed Academic Instruction in English (SDAIE) lessons?

a. Hands-on activities
b. Guarded vocabulary
c. Cooperative learning
d. All of these

55. A teacher has assigned English language learner (ELL) students some English-language text to read as part of a Specially Designed Academic Instruction in English (SDAIE) lesson. The teacher then asks the students to analyze and interpret the text. In what form should the teacher have them give their analyses and interpretations?

a. In written compositions only so they have a chance to organize and edit their ideas
b. In oral class discussions only to avoid writing barriers and give oral language practice
c. In both written and oral form to give equal attention to English language development (ELD) in all four of its domains
d. In individual oral exams only to avoid embarrassment in front of the rest of the class

56. How can teachers best communicate what they expect from English language learner (ELL) students in their English language development (ELD) and content-area performance?

a. Give them a list of expectations in English.
b. Give them a list of expectations in their L1.
c. Give them a clear model of the outcomes.
d. Give them a pretest and then a posttest.

Foundations of ESL Education, Cultural Awareness, and Family and Community Involvement

57. A teacher discovers that an English language learner (ELL) student reacts to certain commonly accepted American hand gestures as insulting and others as indicating different meanings. This is an example of student diversity related to which of these?

a. Internal elements of culture
b. External elements of culture
c. Both internal and external elements of culture
d. Neither internal nor external elements of culture

58. Which contemporary theory bases intergroup bias on a hypothesis of self-esteem?

a. Social identity theory
b. Social dominance theory
c. Terror management theory
d. Optimal distinctiveness theory

59. Among the following cultural contact processes, which is the most associated with loss of one's native culture?

a. Assimilation
b. Biculturalism
c. Acculturation
d. Accommodation

60. When English language learner (ELL) students newly arrive from other countries, in which stage do their parents usually first become alarmed about their children losing their native culture and language?

a. Honeymoon stage
b. Culture shock stage
c. Integration stage
d. Acceptance stage

61. Which of the following is accurate regarding social distance and psychological distance relative to English language learner (ELL) students?

a. Social distance refers to a student's degree of comfort with learning a second language.
b. Psychological distance is a student's degree of contact with a new language community.
c. Psychological distance influences include attitude, integration, and cultural congruence.
d. Social distance is influenced by dominance, enclosure, cohesiveness, residence length.

62. Which of the following represents a major difference in immigration to America after 1965 versus from 1900 to 1965?

a. After 1965, immigrants to America became more likely to arrive from small, rural villages in their nations.
b. After 1965, immigrants to America became more likely to arrive as whole families rather than individuals.
c. After 1965, immigrants to America became more likely to arrive from nations speaking similar languages.
d. After 1965, immigrants to America became more likely to arrive on the US East Coast than the West Coast.

63. A teacher gives students an activity wherein students volunteer one at a time to leave the room and the rest group themselves according to some common characteristic (e.g., eye color, gender, height, nationality). The student who left returns and must guess in which group he or she belongs and state why. If incorrect he or she may not join and must guess again. With every new volunteer, the rest regroup by a different characteristic. Then the class discusses their experiences and feelings. This exercise is designed to help students focus on which of the following?

a. Diversity
b. Exclusion
c. Prejudice
d. Discrimination

64. Among contemporary causes of migration and immigration, which of the following types of causes is most likely to result in involuntary migration to the United States?

a. Educational
b. Economic
c. Political
d. Familial

65. According to research findings, which statement best reflects what is true as English language learner (ELL) students shift from L1 to L2 use?

a. L1 attrition is beneficial to ELL students for their L2 acquisition.
b. L1 maintenance is important for developing L2 vocabulary.
c. L1 maintenance promotes cognitive benefits, pride, and confidence.
d. L1 attrition is not beneficial to ELLs, but (B) and (C) are correct.

Refer to the following for questions 66–67:

> An English learner from China painstakingly writes down everything that she sees on the board and doesn't seem to know how to take notes. She does well on tests and assignments, but she often takes much longer than the rest of her peers during class because of her note-taking skills. Mr. Robinson notices that when he speaks individually with this English learner, the student often does not make eye contact. He wonders if this has to do with cultural differences.

66. What feature of pragmatic language does this student's eye contact behavior relate to?

a. Nonverbal communication
b. Academic language structure
c. Leadership register
d. Family acculturation

67. What is the best explanation for why she takes notes in this fashion?

a. The student is learning how to write English.
b. The student has no ability to discern important information from details.
c. The student is used to the routines of her home country and follows those patterns.
d. The student has poor motor skills and needs writing support.

68. Because of cultural differences in social space, a person from _____ is MOST likely to feel uncomfortable that a person from _____ is standing too close to him or her during a social interaction.

a. Italy; England
b. Norway; Brazil
c. Bulgaria; Estonia
d. Croatia; Vietnam

69. Which of the following is true regarding intercultural communication between someone from America and someone from an East Asian country such as Japan or Korea?

a. The American's manner of speaking could come off as overly direct and shocking to the person from East Asia.
b. The American's manner of speaking could be too subtle and indirect for the person from East Asia.
c. The East Asian's manner of speaking will likely be more direct than the American is used to.
d. The East Asian's manner of speaking will likely be confusing to the American due to being dishonest.

70. Which of the following is most commonly recommended by experts in cultural conflict prevention and resolution?

a. Following the Golden Rule
b. Following the Platinum Rule
c. Refraining from asking questions regarding differences in culture
d. Only recognizing diversity in the presence of multiple cultures

71. A classroom teacher is expecting a new English language learner ELL student recently arrived from a strongly collectivist culture. Which of the following first lesson activities is MOST likely to be culturally congruent for this student?

a. An English literary interpretation
b. A whole-class academic contest
c. An independent study exercise
d. A collaborative learning project

72. A teacher, observing a new English language learner (ELL) student's aversion to making an oral presentation before the class, is trying to determine whether this is caused by a lack of confidence with the English language or lack of personal self-confidence. When she consults with a colleague whether to get the student coaching in EL speaking skills or individual counseling, the colleague suggests the student's attitude could be due to cultural values instead. Investigating, the teacher confirms this. Which factor MOST influenced the teacher's initial attribution of the student's attitude to linguistic or personal rather than cultural causes?

a. The teacher's ignorance about the student's home culture
b. The teacher's own cultural values, beliefs, and assumptions
c. The teacher's own history of lacking confidence in childhood
d. The teacher's lack of familiarity with the student as a person

73. A teacher wants to become more informed about how an individual English language learner (ELL) student's family applies native cultural traditions related to social occasions and interactions. If the teacher were to do only one of the following, which one would be MOST useful for this purpose?

a. Informal conversation with classmates
b. Interviews in this culture's community
c. Home visits with this student's family
d. Reading books on the family's culture

74. Which of the following is the MOST appropriate teacher approach to support cultural diversity and student achievement equally?

a. Communicating higher language expectations for native English speakers and lower ones for English language learners (ELLs)
b. Communicating high expectations of all students, accommodating ELLs culturally and linguistically
c. Communicating overall lower expectations for all students as a means of accommodating the ELLs
d. Communicating high overall expectations of native English-speaking students and lower overall of ELL students

75. Of the following teacher practices, which most demonstrates respect for student cultural and linguistic diversity?

a. The teacher consistently corrects English language learner (ELL) students using L1s by telling them to use English.
b. The teacher uses extinction with L1 use by not responding unless students use the L2.
c. The teacher instructs ELL students to replace cultural tradition with American practices.
d. The teacher shows interest in ELL students' L1s and allows and affirms their use of L1s.

76. Among the following choices, which is MOST advisable for providing a culturally inclusive learning environment in schools?

a. Assigning homogeneous group learning activities so students with similar backgrounds interact
b. Assigning independent learning activities to prevent cultural conflicts during student interaction
c. Assigning cooperative group learning activities for students of different backgrounds to interact
d. Assigning students to fixed pairs so every partner gets exposure to a different background

77. Which of these MOST accurately differentiates characteristics of prejudice versus discrimination?

a. Prejudice involves uninformed opinions, while discrimination involves unfair treatment.
b. Prejudice involves the actions one takes, while discrimination involves what one thinks.
c. Prejudice involves judging ahead of time, while discrimination involves fine distinctions.
d. Prejudice involves exactly the same things that discrimination involves; they are equal.

78. Regarding some ways to involve English language learner (ELL) students' parents in the school, what is recommended?

a. Back-to-school events for parents should be conducted only using English.
b. Organizing school orientation tours should include bilingual facilitators.
c. Parents view informing them of learning opportunities as condescending.
d. Immigrant parents have too much to cope with without volunteering.

79. For inclusive teaching, which of these would give diverse students more flexibility in instruction and assessment?

a. Assigning every student a topic for completing projects
b. Presenting information either orally or visually, not both
c. Weighting all assignments toward final grades in advance
d. Making some assignments individual, some collaborative

80. For making English language learner (ELL) students' parents feel welcome to become engaged with their children's learning, which knowledge would help educators plan how to reach out to them MOST?

a. What educational experiences and backgrounds the parents have had
b. In which language the parents are most comfortable communicating
c. How long the parents have been living in the United States
d. Which work histories and occupations the students' parents have had

Answer Key and Explanations for Test #2

Language Concepts and Language Acquisition

1. A: This is an example of how factors in the context of a discourse influence an individual's choices among variations within a language. Fredo varies the formality of his vocabulary and structural usages according to social distance, that is, speaking more formally with adult authority figures and more informally with friends. This is not an example of regional dialect persistence (B): Fredo came to America from another country rather than relocating within America, and there is no mention of regional dialect. This is not Fredo's English language learner (ELL) status influencing his correct English (C): Neither of the variations he uses with adults or friends is described as having incorrect constructions. Varying speech style according to the persons addressed is not influenced by Fredo's native language (D): This commonly is done by speakers in English and other languages as a sociological phenomenon.

2. C: Physical proximity is a feature of pragmatics, like eye contact, gestures, idiomatic expressions, use of various registers, and so on. Personal and social space and distance vary culturally. In Italy, people stand closer to others when speaking than they do in America; in England, they stand farther apart than they do in America. Physical proximity is not a feature of discourse (A), which involves coherence, cohesion, fluency, structure, and so on, in using language; or semantics (B), which involves the meanings of words and phrases; or social functions of language (D), which are to give information, convince others of an argument or viewpoint, control others' thinking or behavior, or amuse or entertain others.

3. D: Sylvia needs to work on her fluency in oral discourse. Fluency is speaking at an appropriate rate, smoothly, and without pauses or interruptions. Her responsiveness (A) is good: She addresses points classmates have just mentioned. Her coherence (B) is good: She organizes her ideas and unifies her overall message. Her cohesion (C) is good: She finds words and phrase to connect and transition between sentences.

4. D: Academic essays include different text structures, for example, comparison–contrast, problem–solution, logical sequence, attributive, and so on. Giving English language learner (ELL) students examples of these and helping them analyze the essays will familiarize them with the organization, characteristics, and parts of different essay types; helping them make graphic organizers that visually illustrate the various essay types' structures will not only acquaint them with essay formats but will also give them tools they can refer to for writing their own essays. Answer choice A would give writing practice but no exposure to existing academic essay types. Answer choice B would give practice with vocabulary using contextual cues but no familiarity with academic essay text structures. Answer choice C would help ELLs compare but not differentiate essay types.

5. A: How word roots and affixes (i.e., prefixes, infixes, and suffixes) are combined to create words in a language is a feature of morphology. Intonation patterns in speech (B), vocal pitch when speaking (C), and letter–sound relationships (D) or phonics are all phonological features.

6. D: *Calisthenics* has the Greek root *kalos,* meaning beautiful, or *kallos,* meaning beauty. (*Calligraphy* and *kaleidoscope* are from the same root.) *Calorie* (A) comes from the Latin *calor,* meaning heat (*caldron* is from the same source). Calendar (B) is from the Latin *calare,* meaning to call (*class, claim, conciliate, council,* and *nomenclature* are as well). *Calumny* (C) derives from the

Latin *calumnia,* meaning trickery or slander, from *calvi,* meaning to trick or deceive (*cavil* and *challenge* are also from this root).

7. B: The word *calcium*, as well as the words *calcite, calculate, calculus, chalk,* and *recalcitrant,* has dual roots: the Latin *calcis,* the genitive case of *calx,* meaning lime, which originated from the Greek *khalix,* meaning limestone or pebble. While some English words developed directly from one or the other language, some came from Greek earlier and Latin later after the Romans conquered the Greeks during the reign of the Roman Empire and adapted some words from Greek to Latin; others like this one retained two distinct Greek and Latin source words concurrently. *Index* (A) originally is a Latin word meaning one who points out. *Campus* (C) is also Latin, meaning field or level ground. Candle (D) derives from the Latin *candela,* from *candere* meaning to shine.

8. C: *Clavicle,* meaning collarbone, and *clavichord,* a keyboard instrument preceding the piano, both derive from the Greek *kleis,* key, and *kleiein,* to close (these Greek words probably contributed to the later Latin *clavis* and New Latin *clavicula,* the more recent sources of clavicle). *Clinic* comes from the Greek *klinē,* bed, and *klinein*, to recline or lean; *recline* comes from the Latin *re* (back) + *clinare,* to bend (A). Note: The similar sounds and meanings of Greek *klinein* and Latin *clinare* seem to suggest the Latin was adapted from the Greek like many other roots; however, dictionaries give only the Latin root for the words *recline, decline,* and *incline* and only the Greek root for *clinic.* This is related to how the words first entered the English language. *Clause* (B) comes from Latin *clausus* and *claudere,* close or shut; *claustrophobia* (D) is from the same root. *Iconoclast* (D) is from the Greek *klastos,* meaning broken.

9. C: Vocabulary development is most promoted by word analysis informed by knowledge of morphology in this example: These words are all derived from the same Latin roots, *solvere* and *solutus,* meaning to loosen or free and loosened, freed, or unbound. Knowing these two forms of the root, plus the Latin suffix *-tion,* denoting a noun, enables English language learners (ELLs) to expand their vocabulary of related words.

10. C: In Spanish, the letter *h* is silent in all words (including proper names) when it is at the beginning of the word (e.g., Hidalgo, *hacer* [to do or make], *hermosa* [beautiful], etc.) Hence, there is such a letter in the Spanish alphabet (A). There is a similar phoneme in Spanish (B): The letter *j* (and the letter *x* in some proper names and the letter *g* before the letters *e* and *i*) is pronounced /x/—not the same as /h/ because, whereas /h/ is a voiceless glottal fricative, /x/ is a voiceless velar fricative—but somewhat similar in that they are both devocalized fricatives. Some English words also have an initial silent h, like *honest, honor, heir, hour,* and so on. Spanish-speaking students are not generalizing from these words to all English words with initial h (D), however; they are transferring from the silent word-initial h rule in their native language, which is much more familiar to them than any specific English vocabulary words.

11. A: The Texas ELPS for Listening define the Intermediate level for Listening as needing such extensive supports with unfamiliar conversation topics. Needing them with familiar topics (B) is part of the definition of the Beginning level for Listening. Needing them only at times to support understanding (C) is part of the definition of the Advanced level for Listening. Needing them only as exceptions with highly specialized or complex academic language (D) is part of the definition of the Advanced-high level for Listening.

12. C: The error is in subject–verb agreement. The student has included two subjects, "understanding spoken English" and "speaking in English," so the verb should be the plural *are* rather than the singular *is*. There is nothing wrong with the word order (A) or the verb tense (B), only the number. Thus (D) is incorrect.

13. C: This child has not yet mastered the pragmatics feature of register. As dictated by social distance and norms, the expressions he learned from classmates are appropriate for informal use with fellow students but inappropriate for the more formal address required with an adult authority figure. While the expressions in the example are idiomatic (A), the student has indeed mastered them. Setting (B) is not the issue, as idioms are often used in school with classmates, just not with the principal. Purpose (D) is not involved. The student's purpose was to demonstrate his learning of American expressions, which he did; he just used the wrong register, which incorporates these idioms, to address the principal.

14. A: This is mostly an example of using the student's prior knowledge of his native language to promote English language development. The teacher points out and lists L1–L2 cognates, showing same and similar spellings and different pronunciations. The similarity of cognates reinforces Jose's ability to add new English vocabulary words through his familiarity with the Spanish versions of the same words. Explaining and modeling the pronunciation differences help him make adjustments for correctly articulating the English versions. This is not an example of teaching decoding skills (B) as the teacher is not showing him specifically how to associate English letters with English phonemes. It is not systematic phonics instruction (C) for the same reason. It is not applying word analysis (D) because they are not breaking the words down into their component parts or discussing their etymologies.

15. B: Some American villages established in the 17th century by English settlers were surrounded by mountains and forests, making them difficult to access. Dwelling in such relative isolation, the inhabitants were found to have retained certain Elizabethan English speech forms for centuries thereafter. This example reflects a geographical influence on language variations. Answer choice A reflects a political influence on language variations. Answer choice C reflects a cultural influence on language variations. Answer choice D reflects a social influence on language variations.

16. B: Coherence refers to how text is unified and organized overall by using devices like a thesis statement and topic sentences; cohesion refers more specifically to how sentences within a text are connected by using devices like reference, pronouns, repetition, and conjunctions. Hence, they do not mean the same thing (A). Choices C and D are both incorrect.

17. D: School personnel should strike a balance between recognizing and respecting her cultural background, which informs her behavior, and making American cultural norms explicit while gently encouraging her adaptation to them without force or intimidation. Punishing the customary behavior she has learned throughout life (A) is unfair and not an appropriate application of behavioral techniques. Neither is it appropriate or constructive at the other extreme to imitate her behavior in attempts to make her comfortable (B). While explaining the significance of eye contact in the United States—to demonstrate that one is paying attention, show engagement and interest, and connect personally with others—is indicated, assigning her to research and write an essay about it (C) is not: This part of the answer would constitute an unwarranted punitive measure.

18. A: Social interactionist theory proposes that context (the surrounding environment and language used by people in it; world knowledge; and goals, motivating children to use linguistic utterances to attain them) influence language development. As its name indicates, this theory emphasizes social interactions in language acquisition. Behaviorist theory (B) emphasizes the environment's evoking certain responses in the individual through antecedents (preceding stimuli) and consequences (ensuing stimuli) to make a behavioral response more likely to occur and recur. Behaviorism applies these principles to verbal behaviors among all observable behaviors. Cognitive theory (C), like Piaget's theory of cognitive development, is constructivist, proposing individuals actively construct their learning and realities through interacting with and acting upon their environments. Piaget related language development to cognitive stages, each with new abilities developing. Nativist theory (D), like Chomsky's, says that people have innate language acquisition devices (LADs) and universal grammar, enabling rapid language acquisition and generation of endless linguistic combinations.

19. D: While these words do not seem long, complex, or difficult phonologically or morphologically, they are all conceptually abstract. According to cognitive developmental theory like Piaget's, children are not cognitively ready to understand or manipulate abstract concepts until preadolescence or adolescence, when they achieve formal operations. While young, preoperational children (A) have concepts of freedom, truth, beauty, and love, their perceptions of these are very simple, intuitive, and concrete, as evidenced by their definitions of them. Older elementary (B) students are typically in concrete operations, and middle school (C) students are transitioning into formal operations. Out of the grade levels listed, concepts like free will, truth, beauty, and love would be most developmentally appropriate to high school students.

ESL Instruction and Assessment

20. B: Team teaching with a math teacher and an English language arts, English as a second language (ESL), or English language development (ELD) teacher would be most effective for instructing English language learner (ELL) students in a cross-disciplinary unit integrating math and ELD. Peer tutoring (A) would be more applicable when having students with higher English language proficiency (ELP) levels in some or all areas tutor students with lower ELP levels in some or all areas but not to planning and teaching a unit integrating math and ELD instruction. Educational technologies (C) are effective for many purposes, for example, interactive lessons, independent study, multimedia presentations, homework assignments, researching and writing papers, and so on, and can be well used to supplement the unit described for all these activities and more; but for actually planning and teaching a unit integrating math and ELD to ELL students, teachers are needed. Bilingual paraprofessionals (D) are most helpful for bridging communication gaps with ELL students, providing additional one-to-one or small-group instructional support, informing teachers of linguistic differences, and so on, but they cannot necessarily plan and teach a cross-disciplinary unit.

21. B: Realia (A) and manipulatives (C) are both concrete, hands-on objects and materials, which younger children can access and understand more easily. Kindergarten through Grade 1 students will have more difficulty comprehending concepts unless they are accompanied by concrete objects they can see, touch, and manipulate. Analogies (B), that is, comparing one concept to another, are too abstract for children at these ages, as they do not provide anything concrete to help them understand the abstract ideas involved.

22. A: Repetition is one way of modifying language for English language learners (ELLs) without simplifying it. Paraphrasing is another (as long as alternative words and syntax are on levels equal to the originals). Using easier word choices (B) is simplification through modifying vocabulary. Speaking or reading aloud slower (C) is simplification through modifying speed. Exaggerating either the stressed syllables in words or the salient words in sentences (D) is simplification through modifying stress. Modifying intonation also would constitute simplification.

23. B: The inferential level of meaning infers the author's unstated meaning from events (or facts, images, symbols, or patterns) in reading selections; infers the main idea when not explicitly stated; identifies unstated reasons for acts (or statements or thoughts) according to explicit information; identifies implicit relationships; or predicts likely future actions, events, or results. In this example, the student infers from one spouse's dialogue to the other that the story ended happily for them.

Choice (A) represents the literal level of meaning: The student essentially restates the content of the line of dialogue. Choice (C) is at the evaluative level of meaning by drawing a conclusion about the author's purpose or motivation for writing the ending. Choice (D) is also at the evaluative level by drawing a conclusion about the readers' values.

24. A: By calling on the first student to raise a hand, the teacher is not providing enough wait time for English language learner (ELL) students, who often need longer times than native English-speaking students to process the question content, potentially translate it into their L1s and formulate responses in their L1s, and then translate those responses into English before they are ready to raise their hands. All ELLs except those who have attained native-like English language proficiency (ELP) levels typically undergo this process. The question does not provide information to know whether the teacher frames his or her questions appropriately (B) or varies the types of questions he or she asks according to different student language needs (C); he or she may or not do these things. Hence, it is impossible to say whether the teacher needs to do these (D) or already does them.

25. B: The teacher gave implicit instruction in a metalinguistic learning strategy. By providing an example in Spanish of the sentence construction required in English, the teacher enabled the student to compare both languages and relate the understanding of Spanish conditional-subjunctive to an analogous English construction. If the student had been thinking about her own cognitive processes, how languages work in general, or how either Spanish or English works, she would have been using a more metacognitive (A) strategy. She learned a more metalinguistic strategy by directly comparing two languages and equating a grammatical construction in both. This was not a vocabulary (C) strategy, as the student was unfamiliar with both English and Spanish grammatical terms, having never received formal Spanish grammar instruction. It was not a translation (D) strategy, as the Spanish and English terms are cognates; the student would easily recognize their similarity without needing to translate. The problem was that she did not know their grammatical meaning in either language. The teacher's instruction was more implicit than explicit: the teacher did not explain conditional-subjunctive in either language but simply provided a Spanish-language example and let the student infer an equivalent English construction.

26. A: This is an example of declarative memory, which is the kind of memory that accumulates vocabulary words, phrases, and short sentences including idioms. Procedural memory (B) is the kind of memory that governs the process of applying morphological and grammatical rules to produce language. Episodic memory (C) is a subtype of declarative memory that involves remembering autobiographical events and experiences, including their times, places, other contextual elements, and the emotions associated with them. The other subtype of declarative memory is semantic memory, which describes the kind of declarative memory accessed in this example—vocabulary meanings, facts, knowledge, concepts, and so on. Because declarative memory is the only correct choice given, answer choice D is incorrect.

27. D: Providing realia from home countries of English language learner (ELL) students will stimulate students to explain, ask about, and explore characteristics and functions of these objects, generating relevant classroom conversations, which will further student English language development. Realia from other countries will not inform understanding of challenges to immigrant groups in the United States (A) as learning about topics like the naturalization process and discrimination would. Exposure to realia from their own and other students' home countries will not impede US acculturation (B). The objects are in the classroom; students are still exposed to mainstream cultural objects throughout everyday life. Teaching object names in other languages will not interfere with English language development (ELD) in vocabulary (C). The children are conversing about objects in English and are otherwise required to use English inside and outside school. Also, many foreign-language words are sources of English vocabulary words; knowing some of these names can inform and enrich vocabulary knowledge in both other languages and English.

28. C: There is no need for the teacher to abandon his tradition (A) of telling a story for the students' enjoyment. Incorporating a holiday that only some English language learner (ELL) students observe (B) would exclude the other ELL students in the class. The teacher can modify the Thanksgiving celebration to a more universal family occasion, for example, a birthday, the birth of a new baby, and so on. Or he could make it a New Year celebration: Though different cultures may celebrate this on different dates (e.g., the Chinese New Year or Israeli or Jewish New Year), they generally do celebrate it. Continuing the tradition unchanged will enable ELL students to learn about US culture (D), but it will not include the ELL students, which is what the question asks.

29. D: These two groups have differing academic needs. One has been exposed to academic language in their L1s—formal academic paradigms such as verb conjugations, mathematical formulae, scientific inquiry methods, assignments involving reading texts and writing compositions, and so on—the other has not. No information is given to indicate their specific cultural (A), linguistic (B), or cognitive (C) needs differ in these ways. One exception is that, linguistically, the students lacking previous formal education were not exposed to academic language in their L1s; however, learning academic English is a subcategory of learning all procedures associated with formal education, so academic needs is still the better choice.

30. C: Rosetta Stone, a popular language-learning system, has a website with interactive software including live lessons online, community-building activities, games, and more designed to teach learners how to speak foreign languages including English with native-like proficiency. The English as a second language (ESL) Jobs Forum (A) is a website for teachers of ESL to obtain information about training, teacher certification, job openings, and teaching. The Reading Plus system (B) is a web-based program designed to help students in Grade 3 and higher to improve not English speaking but reading proficiency including vocabulary, comprehension, silent reading, fluency, and standardized test scores. Easy Writer, from Software for Students (D), is a software application that uses authentic writing tasks to help English language learners (ELLs) develop their English writing, not speaking, proficiency.

31. A: To develop English language learner (ELL) students' academic English in content-based English language development (ELD) instruction, the teacher needs to expose them to the maximum comprehensible English print materials possible. Selecting a grade-level text will ensure they are learning content appropriate to fifth grade. Adapting the syntax and vocabulary of the textbook to student English language proficiency (ELP) levels will make it comprehensible to them while also furthering their development of academic English. Avoiding print (B) will not give enough written English exposure. Substituting an outline for text (C) also limits print exposure. Selecting a lower grade-level text (D) will not provide appropriate grade-level content.

32. D: The interactive reading model emphasizes both interpretation skills, like making inferences and predictions, and word-level skills, like decoding (A). It regards reading as both proceeding from the parts to the whole (B) and from the whole to the parts (C). The interactive reading approach treats reading as a cognitive process that synthesizes information from both sensory and intellectual elements of reading.

33. B: Research shows that teaching early literacy strategies to English language learner (ELL) students who are refugees with little, interrupted, or no formal education is very effective, enabling them to progress by an average of eight reading levels within a single semester. This technique is not developmentally inappropriate (A) because these students lacked the preliteracy as well as literacy skills needed, even in their native languages (D). This instructional approach not only improved overall student achievement in reading but in receptive and expressive vocabulary as well (C).

34. C: According to the Texas ELPS, ELL students at the Advanced level for writing in English can participate meaningfully in most grade-appropriate shared writing activities if they have second language acquisition (SLA) support. Those who cannot participate meaningfully in these activities (A) are defined as at the Beginning level for writing in English. Those who can only participate meaningfully with very familiar, concrete writing topics using very high-frequency English (B) are designated as at the Intermediate level for writing in English. Those who can participate meaningfully in most grade-appropriate shared writing activities in English (D) are identified as at the Advanced High level for writing in English.

35. C: The reading comprehension process this student has demonstrated most is identifying cause and effect in a text. The student accurately commented that the assassination triggered a series of occurrences leading up to World War I. This is more strongly associated with cause and effect than with making inferences (A) about things not stated in the text. Even if the text did not state the causal relationship explicitly, it arranged the events in chronological order and selected them to show this relationship. This was less related to identifying facts and opinions (B) because the description refers only to events, which presumably were facts, and does not mention any author opinions. The student did not relate any of the events in the text to his or her own experiences (D) in the description.

36. C: This is an example of the revision aspect of the writing process. The student adds needed connective language and deletes verbiage that contributes no additional meaning. Organization (A) would involve things like starting with a thesis statement, beginning paragraphs with topic sentences, paragraphing appropriately to topic changes, and so on. Evaluation (B) would involve the student's coming up with a judgment about the value and effectiveness of his or her own composition. Focus (D) would involve clearly identifying the main point of the composition in advance, plus any supporting or related points, and then avoiding going off the subject by keeping the writing directed at the main point.

37. B: There are no grammatical errors in this sentence. There is a spelling (A) error where the word *first* is misspelled "frist." There are punctuation (C) errors where the comma is omitted following *Washington*, and the periods are omitted from *D.C.*, and there is a capitalization (D) error where *D.C.* is written in lowercase instead of capital letters.

38. D: When teachers plan Specially Designed Academic Instruction in English (SDAIE) lessons, they must include learning objectives for literacy (reading and writing) at grade level in the English language (A), for understanding and using academic English language (both Tier II, general cross-curricular academic English and Tier III, subject-specific terminology) (B), and also for knowing, understanding, analyzing, synthesizing, and evaluating content in the various required academic subjects at grade level (C).

39. B: The student made a connection between his previous knowledge from life experiences and the text he encountered in school because they shared common subject matter. The teacher can take advantage of this in accessing the student's previous knowledge. The teacher did not need to scaffold student–text interactions (A) because the student did not need it in this case. The example illustrates an independent student–text interaction, not a scaffolded teacher–student interaction (C). The teacher did not use strategies to create background knowledge (D), which already existed in this example.

40. D: Younger children are fascinated with real objects (A) and relate more to things they can see, touch, and physically manipulate (B) because their cognitive development is more concrete. Focus questions (C), though also useful when at a developmentally appropriate cognitive level, are still more abstract by nature than concrete objects.

41. A: It is not true that letting students speak in their L1s will interfere with their English language learning (A). Especially when English language learners (ELLs) have not yet attained good English proficiency, letting them communicate in their L1s will promote active use of language (C) and serve as a bridge to communicating in English. Cooperative learning tasks (B) will require students to communicate with one another to complete the work, which will also promote active language use. Adding contextual aids, such as graphic organizers or sentence frames can help promote the English language learners active use of language (D).

42. C: Having the projects be original incorporates creativity; having them solve some problem incorporates critical thinking; having students plan and execute the projects as a joint effort incorporates collaboration and communication. Choice (A) incorporates critical thinking but not the other three Cs. Choice (B) incorporates critical thinking, collaboration, and communication in the planning stage but not in the execution stage. Choice (D) incorporates creativity and critical thinking, but it does not incorporate collaboration and communication in the planning stage. Thus, only (C) incorporates all four Cs throughout the entire activity.

43. A: To access students' prior knowledge, the most effective scaffolding strategy of the choices offered is to relate the new concepts and vocabulary words in English to ideas that are culturally familiar to English language learner (ELL) students and to equivalent or similar words in their native languages. Comparing the concepts to similar concepts that are also new in English and offering multiple word synonyms that are also English (B) do not access prior student knowledge: These only relate new material to other new material. Visual aids (C) are helpful for illustrating new concepts and words but may or may not access prior student knowledge depending on whether the visuals are familiar to them. Similarly, hands-on activities wherein students apply the new concepts and words (D) may or may not access their prior knowledge depending whether anything in the activities is familiar to them.

44. D: The question in (A) requires only factual knowledge, that is, remembering (or looking up) and reciting the seven names of noble gases. Question (B) requires this same factual knowledge plus being able to categorize gases and differentiate noble gases from other kinds. Question (C) is similar to question (B) but is also outdated and inaccurate for using the term *inert*: Noble gases historically were considered inert but today are deemed relatively inert, that is, extremely stable and nonreactive, but it is not completely impossible for them to form compounds as previously thought. Question (D) requires the most critical thinking because students must apply knowledge of the stability of noble gases to answer "easy" or "hard" and then must additionally explain why, that is, because their octets or valence shells are filled with the maximum numbers of electrons, making them very stable and thus resistant to compounding. This question requires analysis, application, and interpretation as well as factual knowledge.

45. A: To frontload vocabulary, that is, pre-teach English language learners (ELLs) the vocabulary words used in a text that they will need to know in order to understand it before they read it, the first thing teachers need to do is to scan the text to identify the vocabulary words most likely to cause problems for these students. Research has revealed that, to comprehend text, students need a working knowledge of 95%—that is, most—of its vocabulary, not just 75% (B), so front-loading can be crucial for ELLs. An enormous help for identifying problem words in advance is to obtain student

Lexile reading levels (C), which will give teachers an indication of which vocabulary they are likely to know and not know. Lexile Analyzer also will help teachers select specific texts (D) by scanning texts and returning their readability levels.

46. B: Research studies have found that giving English language learner (ELL) students explicit instruction in text genres in English helps them to improve their English writing skills. Hence, option A is incorrect. Studies also show that working with genres does help students to focus on text (C). Changing the genre of a given text to another genre involves producing a whole text, which is found to benefit both ELL and native English-speaking students (D).

47. B: The teacher should group English language learner (ELL) and native English-speaking students heterogeneously to give ELL students authentic opportunities to use English to communicate regarding academic content with both native and non-native English speakers. They should not be grouped homogeneously (A) as this will restrict their academic English communication to being only with other non-native English speakers. In some cases, it may be reassuring and supportive to place at least two ELLs per heterogeneous group (C), but this is not always necessary and, in some classes, can be impossible depending on numbers of students. As heterogeneous grouping will give ELLs opportunities to communicate with both native and non-native English speakers and homogeneous grouping will not, it is incorrect that the grouping will make no difference (D).

48. A: Long-term ELs, born in the United States to immigrant parents speaking only their native languages, have attended US schools all their lives but with instruction so inadequate that their English skills—spoken, academic, or both—prevent school success. Under-schooled ELs, despite being in higher school grades, have had inadequate or interrupted instruction or have missed earlier grades in their home countries or the United States. Generation 1.5 ELs were born in another country, came to the United States around 12 years old and began American education in middle or high school. By the time they are high school seniors, they have been educated in the United States for 6 to 10 years. Thus, long-term ELs and Generation 1.5 ELs are likely to have spent more total time being educated in the United States. While some under-schooled ELs may have had equally long US educations that were extremely inadequate, many others in this population have missed a lot of school, so this group overall is less likely to have as much total US education time, and answer choice D is less likely.

49. A: A summative assessment is best for evaluating whether students have attained the state standards that the instruction was designed to meet. Evaluating students' progress during instruction (B), determining how to modify instruction to make it more effective (C), and designing further differentiated, standards-based instruction for given students (D) are all more appropriately evaluated by using formative assessments.

50. D: The Texas ELPS state that ELLs at the Beginning level of ELP will get little or no meaning from hearing grade-appropriate stories read aloud to them in English *unless* the stories are read in short "chunks" or segments rather than the whole story in one reading. The stories must also be controlled to include only what little English these students know, which is high-frequency, concrete, and recently practiced (A). Additionally, read-aloud stories must include plentiful visual supports like illustrations, gestures, objects, and pantomime (B); and linguistic supports like slower than normal speech and more careful than usual enunciation (C). All these conditions are needed for Beginning-level ELLs to get any meaning from read-aloud stories.

51. A: Backward Design differs from other instructional planning processes in that teachers have to plan a variety of assessments before they plan learning activities; they do not develop both at the same time (B); they do not plan lessons before assessments, and the authors advise assessment throughout the learning sequence, not only at its end (D). While they emphasize authentic performance tasks, the authors recommend balancing these with tests, quizzes, observation, and other more traditional assessments rather than replacing the latter with the former (C).

52. B: This is primarily an issue of test reliability, because the test does not yield similar results across repeated administrations with the same ELL students. While such a pattern might prompt further investigation of possible test bias or fairness issues, bias typically refers to systematic advantages or disadvantages for particular groups, not just inconsistent scores. Validity (A) is the ability of a test to measure what it claims and intends to measure. While the varying reliability of the test described between native English-speaking versus English language learner (ELL) students is likely due to test bias (C) in favor of the former and to the latter's detriment; still the fact that it does not obtain similar results across repeated administrations with the same ELL students makes it primarily an issue of reliability. The main issue is not how the test is administered (D), but rather the reliability.

53. A: The excessive number of idiomatic expressions is an example of test bias. Only native English-speaking students would understand these idioms. The test would only be unreliable (B) if it did not get the same or similar results across repeated administrations to the same students. It would be invalid (C) only if it did not test what it claimed or meant to test. It did not reveal a weakness of the ELLs (D); idioms are known to be more difficult than other language features for foreign learners because they often do not make literal sense and require familiarity with each expression for understanding (unless their L1s have similar idioms they are informed of for comparison). Given enough contextual information, some ELLs can figure out what idioms mean but, without knowing their origins, often cannot see or remember the connection between words and meaning.

54. D: Hands-on activities (A) give English language learner (ELL) students authentic contexts for students to learn subject-area content while also developing their English language skills. Guarded vocabulary (B) simplifies English language to enable ELL students to connect new subject content to their first languages and prior experiences. Cooperative learning (C) enhances two-way communication with peers for academic learning purposes.

55. C: English language learner (ELL) students should have text analysis and interpretation assignments as part of Specially Designed Academic Instruction in English (SDAIE) lessons in both written and oral form to develop the listening, speaking, and writing as well as reading domains of English language development (ELD). Therefore, these assignments should not be limited to writing (A) or listening and speaking (B). Individual oral exams with the teacher (D) with the excuse of avoiding student embarrassment will deprive them of the experience and practice they need with using conversational and academic English to listen and speak, that is, communicate, with their peers as well as their teachers.

56. C: The best way for teachers to communicate to English language learner (ELL) students what they expect of their performance in English language development (ELD) and content-area subjects is to provide them with clear models of the outcomes they should become able to achieve. Modeling both surmounts language barriers and provides authentic demonstration; written English does neither (A), and written L1 (B) does the former but not the latter. A pretest and then a post-test (D) will establish what students knew and could do before the instruction and what they know and can do after the instruction, but they will not communicate to students what they will be expected to know or be able to do before or during instruction.

Foundations of ESL Education, Cultural Awareness, and Family and Community Involvement

57. A: Some hand gestures and body postures commonly accepted in America are viewed as insulting or prohibited in other cultures. Others are used in both cultures but convey different meanings. Nonverbal communication is an example of an internal element of culture. External elements of culture (B) include governments, religious structures, languages, technologies, food, clothing, and shelter. Therefore, options C and D are incorrect.

58. A: Social identity theory bases intergroup bias on a need for positive self-esteem, which in-group members derive from positive social identities. Social dominance theory (B) bases intergroup bias on social dominance orientation (SDO): Individuals with high SDO promote in-group domination of out-groups and intergroup hierarchies. Terror management theory (C) bases intergroup bias on a need for self-preservation: Individuals evaluate in-group members positively for holding similar cultural worldviews and out-group members negatively for threatening these. Optimal distinctiveness theory (D) bases intergroup bias on a need to assimilate and an equal, opposing need to differentiate: Individuals identify with groups offering the best balance of the two.

59. A: Assimilation refers to adjusting to a new culture by adopting its characteristics in favor of one's native cultural characteristics, being more or less absorbed into the new culture. Biculturalism (B) involves retaining elements of one's native culture while also adopting elements of the new culture, such that one identifies with two distinct cultures. Acculturation (C) is the process of adjusting and becoming acclimated to a new culture without necessarily assimilating into it or discarding one's native cultural elements. Accommodation (D) is a process of adding elements of a new culture into one's repertoire, adjusting native elements to allow elements of both cultures to coexist compatibly. Native cultural elements may be modified in admitting new cultural elements rather than being replaced by them as in assimilation.

60. C: In the honeymoon (A) or euphoric stage, English language learner (ELL) students are excited to learn about their new environment. In the culture shock stage (B), they become overwhelmed as they begin to realize all the cultural differences and have difficulty coping with surroundings and linguistic and social signals they cannot comprehend. In the integration stage (C), ELL students begin integrating new cultural elements. Some replace old values with new ones; others find ways to maintain both in peaceful coexistence. This is the stage wherein many immigrant parents first become alarmed about their children losing their original values and traditions. In the acceptance (D) stage, ELLs accept and may combine both cultures and can interact comfortably in mainstream culture. In this stage, many immigrant parents try to prevent their children from adopting mainstream culture for fear they will reject or forget their native cultures, which often happens.

61. D: Social distance, not psychological distance (B), refers to a student's degree of contact with a new language community. Psychological distance, not social distance (A), refers to a student's degree of comfort with learning a new language. Psychological distance is influenced by factors including student motivation, culture shock, language shock, and individual ego permeability. Social distance is influenced by factors including student attitude, integration patterns, and cultural congruence (C), as well as social dominance, enclosure, cohesiveness, size, and the student's expected length of residence (D).

62. B: In 1965, the Immigration Act did away with the United States' former quota system, which had prevented many members of Asian, African, and other countries not in Europe from coming to America in larger numbers. The new law favored keeping families together by allowing immigration on a first-come, first-served basis; therefore, after 1965, whole families were more likely to come to the United States than individuals. This law did not affect emigration from urban versus rural areas (A). Because many Asian, African, and Middle Eastern languages were spoken by non-European immigrants, more people arrived speaking languages dissimilar to English, making choice C incorrect. Many Chinese and other Asian immigrants settled in San Francisco and other places on the West Coast, making choice D incorrect.

63. B: This exercise is designed to help students focus on exclusion: how we behave as part of a group, how it feels to reject outsiders, how it feels to be excluded, and when including some people and excluding others becomes a problem. This is not an activity focusing on diversity (A), that is, the differences among people; on prejudice (C), that is, biased opinions about groups or individuals based not on facts but on judgments; or on discrimination (D), that is, behaviors treating others unequally based on race, ethnicity, gender, class, sexual orientation, religion, and so on.

64. C: When people come to the United States from other countries to obtain better or more education (A), it is more often voluntary. When they migrate to find better-paying jobs or more sources of employment (B), some moves may be considered involuntary in the sense that they would rather stay in their home countries but cannot earn enough to support their families. However, the pursuit of better work opportunities is still largely a voluntary reason for coming to America. When people move to America from other countries to be nearer to their family members (D) living here, these are generally voluntary moves. When people come to America fleeing terrorist regimes, to escape political persecution or imprisonment, to live in the greater political freedom of a democratic nation, or for other political (C) reasons, these are most often involuntary moves.

65. D: Research finds that losing their L1s does not benefit English language learner (ELL) students in acquiring the L2 (A). To the contrary, studies show that maintaining the L1 is important to aid ELL students for developing their vocabularies in the L2 (B), for the cognitive benefits they derive from bilingualism, and for the pride and self-confidence (C) they derive from retaining their original languages as they acquire a new one.

66. A: Nonverbal communication includes how one holds oneself along with eye contact and gestures. Cultures have different body language and nonverbal skills that are normalized. In some cultures, eye contact can be seen as disrespectful. Academic language structure refers to the actual vocabulary, syntax, and structure of the language being used. Leadership register is a pragmatic feature that is associated with language used to denote leadership, which often includes commands. Family acculturation is a sociocultural factor that influences student behavior, but it relates to how a family adapts to a new culture and their attitudes toward the dominant culture.

67. C: Each country has its own classroom and school routines. In certain countries, copying down exactly what the teacher has written is expected of students, whereas in others, taking no notes down is expected. It is important that teachers explicitly teach classroom routines related to language functions. This might include explicitly teaching note-taking skills and what is expected of students regarding taking notes. This student probably does not have poor motor skills, nor is she learning to write English because she seems to be doing well on her assessments.

68. B: Different cultures dictate different comfortable distances in social interactions. According to Lewis's Model of Cultural Types, Linear-Active cultures are cool, decisive, factual planners. These include England (A), the United States, Norway (B), Sweden, Germany, Estonia (C), and others. They tend to stand farther apart than Multi-Active cultures, which are emotional, impulsive, warm, and talkative. These include Italy (A), Greece, Spain, Brazil (B), Mexico, Russia, Croatia (D), and others. They stand closer when talking or interacting. Reactive cultures are polite, accommodating, compromising, and good listeners. These include China, Japan, Korea, Vietnam (D), Thailand, the

Philippines, and so on. India is halfway between Multi-Active and Reactive, Canada halfway between Linear-Active and Reactive, and Belgium and Israel halfway between Linear-Active and Multi-Active. Hence, a Norwegian would likely be most uncomfortable if a Brazilian were standing too close during an interaction. The other choices are all the reverse of this relationship.

69. A: Americans tend to use more direct language than those from East Asian cultures, which often convey meaning through more indirect statements and nonverbal cues. Some people from East Asia could view American speech as shockingly direct or insensitive. Some East Asian cultures, such as Japan, prioritize the avoidance of direct conflict over the facilitation of direct expression. These differences should be taken into account during intercultural communication.

70. B: Experts in cultural conflict prevention and resolution say that, rather than following the Golden Rule (A) (treating others the way we would like to be treated), it is better to follow the Platinum Rule (treating others the way they would like to be treated). This avoids conflict when the ways of different groups vary. Experts also advise that rather than a "when in Rome, do as the Romans do" approach, that is, conforming unquestioningly (C) to show respect, it is better to ask questions in an inquiry approach to learn about other cultures and to encourage growth and creativity rather than conformity, which excludes newcomers. They also remind us diversity is not only among different cultures (D) but within cultures; for example, they characterize the two biggest cultural groups as women and men. They find it more productive to assume all communications are cross-cultural in nature.

71. D: Because the new student is an English language learner (ELL), the teacher needs to assess the student's level of English language proficiency (ELP) before assigning interpretation of English literature (A). An academic contest (B) is a competitive activity that would not be congruent culturally for a student from a strongly collectivist culture that values cooperation above competition. Independent study (C) is more suited to the American individualist culture than to the group emphasis of a collectivist culture. A collaborative learning project (D) emphasizes group interdependence, which would be most culturally congruent for this student.

72. B: The teacher initially attributed the student's attitude to either linguistic or personal issues and overlooked the possibility of cultural causes because of her own cultural values, beliefs, and assumptions. This is why it is important for educators to examine their own cultural attitudes and what impacts they have on teaching culturally diverse students. Ignorance about the student's home culture (A) was a secondary reason; however, even not knowing about it, the teacher would more likely consider culture as a reason initially or investigate cultural reasons first were it not for her own cultural assumptions. The question does not include any information about the teacher's own childhood history (C). Knowing the student as a person (D) might or might not show the teacher the student was otherwise self-confident or comfortable with English-language speaking, but only by examining her own cultural assumptions could she consider culture as informing the student's attitude.

73. C: If the teacher wants to know specifically how an individual student's family observes cultural traditions related to social occasions and interactions, home visits with the family (including the student) would allow the teacher both to observe their practices and to interview, ask questions, and converse with the family members about their customs. Informal conversation with the student could elicit the desired information, but conversing with the student's classmates (A) would not yield the same specific information and observations as visiting with the actual student and family and neither would interviewing other members of the culture's community (B). Reading books on the culture (D) would not inform the teacher of one family's specific practices as well as the family itself could.

74. B: Teachers can best support cultural diversity and student achievement equally by communicating equally high expectations of all students, which does not preclude providing appropriate cultural and linguistic accommodations to facilitate English language learner (ELL) student success. This is more effective than lowering expectations for ELLs in language (A), overall (D), or lowering expectations for all students to accommodate ELLs (C).

75. D: By showing interest in English language learner (ELL) students' L1s, allowing them to use their L1, and affirming it, the teacher most demonstrates respect for their cultural and linguistic diversity. Constantly correcting L1 use by telling them to use English (A) denies their linguistic diversity. Ignoring student L1 communications and selectively responding only to L2 use (B) does the same. Instructing ELLs to replace their cultural traditions with American practices (C) disrespects their cultural diversity.

76. C: Assigning cooperative group learning activities allows students of different backgrounds the highest levels of interaction for the most culturally inclusive learning environment. Assigning students to homogeneous groups with similar backgrounds (A) reduces interaction with students from other backgrounds. Assigning independent activities to prevent cultural conflicts (B) eliminates learning interactions with students from diverse backgrounds. Assigning students to fixed pairs to expose each student to one partner's different background (D) limits each student to learning interactions with only one other student from a different background, instead of with many other students from different backgrounds.

77. A: Prejudice involves forming opinions of groups or individuals without any knowledge about them; discrimination involves treating certain groups or individuals differently than others in an unfair way. Prejudice more often involves thoughts; discrimination more often involves actions, not vice versa (B). Judging ahead of time is a literal meaning of the roots of the word *prejudice*; discrimination involving fine distinctions is a valid but separate meaning of the word *discrimination* or *discriminating* (C), as in matters of aesthetic tastes or sensibilities not applying to cultural conflict or treatment of other people. Prejudice and discrimination are related but are not exactly the same (D).

78. B: Experts advise that, to involve the parents of English language learner (ELL) students in the school, educators can arrange back-to-school events. When many parents in a community speak the same non-English language, for example, Spanish in many communities, they advise hosting Spanish-language back-to-school evenings for these parents, including an interpreter, rather than holding them only in English (A). Similarly, school orientation tours for parents should include bilingual facilitators (B) to help communicate school information and answer parent questions. Many recent immigrant parents do not yet know of adult learning opportunities in which they may be interested, including English and native-language literacy classes; teachers can inform them of these without being perceived as condescending (C). Some ELL parents are able, willing, and interested in volunteering at the school (D). Teachers can recruit such parents according to their skills and interests as a way to involve them in the school.

79. D: By varying assignments among individual and collaborative work, a teacher can provide students with more flexibility in how they are assessed. Rather than assigning every student a project topic (A), the teacher can give them multiple topics from which they may choose for more flexibility. To accommodate different backgrounds, experiences, learning styles, and abilities, teachers can present information both orally and visually rather than only one or the other way (B). Rather than weighting all assignments toward final grades in advance (C), teachers can let students decide what percentage of their final grade they want each assignment to contribute at the beginning of the term or school year.

80. B: The most useful thing to know about English language learner (ELL) students' parents for making them feel welcome to become engaged with their children's educations is in which language they feel most comfortable communicating. By knowing this, educators can arrange for bilingual teachers or interpreters to be available so that parents are able to communicate most effectively and naturally during school visits and events. This knowledge has more practical application for interacting with parents than knowing their educational backgrounds (A), length of US residence (C), or work histories and occupations (D).